Delia Smith is Britain's best-selling cookery author. Her books include *Delia Smith's Cookery Course*, *One is Fun*, *Book of Cakes*, *Delia Smith's Summer Collection*, *Delia Smith's Winter Collection* and *Journey into God*. She is also Consultant Food Editor of Sainsbury's The Magazine. She is married to the writer and editor Michael Wynn Jones and they live in Suffolk.

Frugal Food

Delia Smith

CORONET BOOKS
Hodder and Stoughton

First published in Great Britain in 1976 by
Hodder & Stoughton Ltd

New edition 1987

This edition published in 1997 by Hodder and Stoughton
A division of Hodder Headline PLC

A Coronet paperback

10 9 8 7 6 5 4 3 2

Illustrations by Vanessa Pancheri

ISBN 0 340 71294 5

Typeset by Hewer Text Composition Services, Edinburgh
Printed and bound in Great Britain by
Clays Ltd, St Ives plc

Hodder and Stoughton
A division of Hodder Headline PLC
338 Euston Road
London NW1 3BH

All author's royalties from the sale of this book will go to Christian Aid and the Catholic Fund for Overseas Development.

My thanks to Colin Fisher of the Pye Research Centre, Haughley, Suffolk, for his invaluable comments: to Gwyneth Phillips for typing the manuscript: and, as always, to Caroline Liddell for her help with the testing.

CONTENTS

Preface   9

Introduction   11

The Cheap Charter   13

Luxury Soups   19

Eggs and Us   35

Frugal Fish   51

Chickens' Lib   69

Forequarter Front   83

Offal–But I Like You   109

Bangers Are Beautiful   127

Cook for Victory   141

Go with the Grain   155

Who Needs Meat?!   167

Quickening Pulses   181

Back to Baking   195

Pauper's Puddings   207

Conversion Chart   223

Index   225

PREFACE

You may be wondering how it is that a cookery writer who spends a great deal of her time encouraging people to eat perhaps a little more adventurously than they normally would could at the same time have any leanings towards frugality. The fact is I feel our days of unrestricted choice in eating are strictly numbered. There simply isn't enough food on this planet to feed all the people who live on it: rich nations like our own are just beginning to feel the pinch, while two-thirds of the world's population continues to suffer from the grave effects of living below subsistence level.

It is a paradox which concerns me personally a great deal. Ultimately perhaps the problems will have to be solved on an international level, but governments only reflect the will of the people they govern. As individuals, are there really any of us who, if we found ourselves living next door to a family whose children were starving, would not give all the help we could? But the truth is we *are* living next door, on the next continent, on the same planet.

This book has been prompted partly by these considerations and partly by the practical point that in the future there will be less food around (at least of the kind we have been accustomed to)—something that is not entirely unwelcome. One doesn't have to be a nutritionist to realise that our eating habits have got somewhat out of hand, with obesity and the diseases attributable to it having reached epidemic proportions. I feel the positive effect of this in time will be a material improvement in our health, as in the war years when we ate so much less. Also, believe it or not, I do feel that the less you have of something, the more special it is—so you enjoy it more. We shall still be well-off compared with the greater part of the world, which is not to say that we should feel guilty about cooking good food but rather that we should have some sort of responsibility to make the most of it and not squander it.

INTRODUCTION

Anyone who wants to, or is forced to, live *really* frugally (that is to say, at subsistence level) has no need of a cookbook. And at the same time I'm quite sure there are many people who, because they are careful, can live more frugally than this book would suggest.

Who, then, is this book for? Quite simply for people like myself, those who have lived and cooked during the affluent years and now find themselves caught up in the spiral of inflation, rising prices and impending world food shortages.

In short, it's a *start*. If you wish to trim your cooking (and spending) wings a bit, start here. It's quite easy, quite fun and, if my experience in preparing and writing this book is anything to go by, it's really not half so morbid an exercise as you might think. In fact, once you become really calculating, boring old shopping can take on a new meaning.

No more will you simply go through the motions of loading up the supermarket trolley and day-dreaming in dreary check-out queues. You'll go forth into battle fortified, as it were, by the armour of your new-found attention to frugality! The seductive cunning of commercials will now meet its match—in you. Nothing will be tossed lightly into your basket: you'll know how much it weighs, what it costs, *and* how much it cost last week.

You haven't got the time? I know, I said it too. But suddenly I didn't have the money to save all this time we've become so besotted with. Actually I'm not so sure that all this time-saving really does save time. I once watched a lady standing in a long check-out queue with just a large bag of frozen Brussels sprouts (they were at the time about 30 per cent dearer than the fresh ones). She was in the queue for a good 10 or 12 minutes; she could, had she so wished, have sat in her own kitchen and peeled fresh Brussels sprouts in the same time. Then take something like tea bags: they'll save you the bother of emptying tea leaves—whatever small amount of time that involves—but you'll pay twice the price for your tea.

However, before we start cooking, here are a few tips on thinking frugally.

THE CHEAP CHARTER

1 *Your money or your time* Really this is what is at the root of many of our economic predicaments. 'Labour-saving' was the slogan of the 'sixties: leave it all to the kitchen gadgets, the machines, the tins and packets, and put your feet up. Well, even if you overlook the psychological repercussions for bored (if liberated) housewives, consider the economic implications for a minute. First of all, instant foods cost a fortune. Secondly, all those super gadgets cost a fortune—and then they break down, and when they do it's ten to one you can't get the mending-man to come. 'Are you north or south Suffolk,

madam?' 'Oh, you're in the middle. He won't be in your area for ten days.' So off you go to the launderette, get a parking ticket, plus the call-out charge for the repair man when he comes ten days later and the cost of the spare part. Just one (real-life) example of how much saved labour we have to pay for. The same applies to cooking: if you are willing to spend the *time*, you are bound to save money.

2 *Getting out of the supermarket and back into the kitchen* So our bored, liberated housewife needs a job (*a*) to pay for her labour-saving home and (*b*) to pay the interest. With the result that on Friday nights and Saturdays the supermarkets are packed with rushed, harassed, working wives and mothers stocking up on instant puds, apple pies, sponge cakes, frozen hamburgers, fish fingers and packaged meat, to name but a few expensive items. A few years ago I wrote a book to enable people to make the very best of all these things. But in the meantime our priorities, I feel, have been changing, and it is the kitchen now that demands more of our time and imagination. Hence the aim of this book—to make that time spent as interesting and worthwhile as possible.

3 *Seasonal sense* I need hardly mention how the price of oil has affected everything we consume, but just *think* how much more it now costs to fly all those tasteless out-of-season fruits and vegetables merely so we can choose whatever we want every single week of the year! Not only has all this jet-set food eclipsed the natural cycles of our diet, but also it has become so much harder to decide what to cook when there's absolutely everything to choose from. Nature is perfectly capable of providing us with a varied and interesting diet throughout the year, and by buying things in their natural season you'll be getting them at their most plentiful and therefore at their cheapest. In June a few ungraded asparagus spears can be far cheaper than imported celery; in December home-grown celery is much less expensive (and has far more flavour) than a pound of imported tomatoes. And, personally, I enjoy the fun of anticipation—I long for the first tender young peas, and

equally I look forward to the (so underrated) root vegetables of winter.

4 *Anti freeze* Well, I'm afraid I am, although I admit it's a personal thing largely for the reasons outlined above. Also I'm not convinced freezing does always save money. Each time I am reminded that 20 per cent of the population are freezer-owners I console myself with the thought that there are still 80 per cent who are not. My main grumble is that unless you understand temperature control with almost scientific dedication freezing causes *loss of flavour*, and as a cook I spend a great deal of time and effort nurturing flavour. One report in a consumer magazine pointed out that very often freezer families spent more on meat than other families—they bought more than they normally would in order to justify the freezer, and of course when buying whole sides they were landed with far more heads, tails and ears than they needed. Having said all this, it is true you *can* save a little money with fruit and vegetables, if you grow these yourself and produce too much for your immediate needs. If you already have a freezer and it's saving you money, it can't be a bad thing. On the other hand, if you don't have one and are thinking about it, do ask yourself if you really want to eat your courgettes and strawberries in January and your red cabbage in June.

5 *Saving it* Energy has become a fashionable word of late. Before that saving kitchen energy meant sitting down to shell the peas. When the Government first urged us daily to switch something off, we listened a bit; then the enormous increases in charges started arriving through our letter-boxes and we listened a lot. After water and heating, the oven is the highest consumer of energy in the house, and heating up the whole capacity of the oven just to cook a quiche is no longer feasible. No doubt you all have devised ways of saving energy in the kitchen, but here anyway are a few suggestions.

(*a*) Keep the kettle regularly de-scaled—it will boil quicker.

(b) Invest in a steamer and cook one vegetable on top of another on the same heat.

(c) When baking jacket potatoes, push a skewer through the centres as this conducts the heat to the insides and speeds up the cooking time.

(d) Invest in an electric toaster—it uses far less energy than the grill.

(e) Try to use the oven to its capacity by planning to use it for more than one thing (e.g. baking in a batch, cooking two casseroles or cooking vegetables and soups in the oven if it's on).

(f) If you are buying a new oven, consider a double one so that you can use the smaller oven for most things and probably cut costs by half.

6 *A touch of spice* One way to prevent life getting dull when you're saving money on cooking is to stock up with a few herbs and spices. Don't get me wrong: throwing in a hotch-potch of this and that is definitely not recommended. It is the subtle addition that adds a touch of luxury to the simplest dishes. First and foremost (I'll say it yet again), do invest in a pepper-mill. Freshly ground black pepper adds a new dimension instantly to your cooking. Also keep some untreated pure rock salt (such as Maldon) in your spice cupboard—it's more expensive than table salt but, because it's saltier, it goes further. Coarsely ground black pepper and a sprinkling of crushed rock salt can put something like egg and chips in the four-star class! Spices are cheaper sold loose or in packets. Why pay for fancy jars? At the same time pester your local delicatessen or wholefood shop for unusual spices—the more we ask, the more we're likely to get them.

Green-fingered cooks, or even those who aren't (like me), should be able to grow fresh herbs, either in the garden or on a sunny windowsill in pots. There are a number of very informative books available.

Finally, one thing that I used to get a lot of letters about was olive oil and its price. It *is* delicious, but I agree that it is very expensive. A good alternative is groundnut oil, which I like because it has little flavour of its own and therefore doesn't mask other flavours, like some abominable oils on the market at present. Groundnut oil is good for frying—and add a knob of butter for flavour.

I also use groundnut oil in salad dressing and in mayonnaise with a little crushed garlic added, again for flavour. If you have some precious olive oil, you can make it go further by adding 50 per cent groundnut oil to it. For my vinaigrette dressing I use 1 tablespoon of wine or cider vinegar, 6–7 tablespoons of oil, 1 crushed clove of garlic, 1 teaspoon of mustard, 1 teaspoon of crushed rock salt and freshly milled black pepper—then I shake everything together vigorously in a screw-top jar. In the summer a few chopped herbs will give it an extra-special flavour.

7 *How to cook without wine*   I think it was Elizabeth David, one of our greatest cookery writers, who once said that if the British spent as much money on wine in the kitchen as they do on gravy powder, meat cubes and instant stock they would all enjoy better food. Well, I heartily endorse that, but just as all those chemically flavoured aids have gone up in price, so too has wine. But, again prompted by Mrs David, I have discovered that a very good alternative to wine in the kitchen is dry cider. In fact, I now rarely use wine, but I always have some dry cider handy for special dishes. I've experimented quite a lot and have found that a classic coq au vin or even boeuf bourguignonne (see the version on page 87) has turned out beautifully with dry cider.

8 *A question of cream*   As a cookery writer I can say quite confidently that nothing seems to get people's economical backs up quite as much as cream in cooking. It's perfectly all right to spend money on smoking, or crisps, or bars of chocolate, but cooking with cream is considered by some to be the

ultimate in kitchen extravagance. One lady was outraged, I recall, by my making a bread and butter pudding on television with cream; I ought to have been teaching people to economise in this day and age. Well, perhaps in the context of this book the appearance of a little cream here and there does call for an explanation. For me, quite simply, cream is the one ingredient that makes frugality tolerable! If you like, you can substitute top of the milk for it.

9 *What are we leaving?*   In one American university there is, would you believe, a department of Garbageology which regularly 'borrows' people's dustbins and analyses their contents. They claim that it tells us a great deal about our modern way of life. In one American city they discovered that the average family wasted 10–15 per cent of all the food it bought (amounting in the whole city, over the year, to $10 million worth of food thrown away). And that was not bones, scraps or peelings but large pieces of once perfectly edible bread and meat, as well as unopened packs of vegetables and television dinners. They even found that, as the price of meat soared, so did the wastage! I mention all this only to underline the obvious point that frugality calls for good management, and an enthusiastic approach to leftovers (for which you'll find some recipes later). It would be a tragic waste of that extra time we're going to spend in the kitchen if 15 per cent of the food was thrown away afterwards.

Luxury SOUPS

So how can we be at once frugal and luxurious, you're thinking? Easy. Luxuries are rarities—foie gras and caviare cost a fortune because they're scarce. When oysters were ten-a-penny (as indeed they were in the last century) they were merely food of the poor: now they're right up in the luxury class.

One of the rarest things in these days of instant living, in my opinion, is real homemade soup made with real homemade stock—and for me that makes it a luxury. At least this state of affairs has a positive side for us frugal cooks, because now we can offer our family or friends luxury at a very small cost.

I'll go even further. If you've got an attractive tureen full of comforting, inviting homemade soup on the table—with homemade bread, butter, a hunk of cheese and some fruit—who's going to notice the absence of meat or fish or any other main course? In this chapter I've chosen, for the most part, substantial and filling soups, and just a couple of lighter ones with the summer months in mind.

Basic Stock

4 lb (1.8 kg) beef shin bones (in pieces)
1 lb (450 g) veal knuckle bones (in pieces)
1 Spanish onion, peeled and quartered
2 large carrots, peeled and cut into large chunks
2 celery stalks (plus leaves), cut into halves
1 bayleaf
1 blade of mace
10 whole black peppercorns
1 small bunch parsley stalks
1 heaped teaspoon salt
1 level teaspoon sugar

Pre-heat the oven to mark 8/450°F/230°C

First of all place the bones in a meat roasting tin together with the onion and carrot, and place the tin on the highest shelf in the oven and leave it for about 45 minutes to allow the bones and vegetables to brown—turning them now and then so that they brown evenly. Then have some boiling water ready, and transfer the bones, the onion and carrots to a cooking pot (about 6 quarts or 12 pints/6.8 litres capacity).

Add 7 pints (4 litres) of water to the pot, along with the celery, bay leaf, mace, peppercorns and parsley stalks, and bring the liquid very slowly up to simmering point before adding the salt and sugar. Skim off any scum that has come to the surface, partly cover and simmer as gently as possible for 4 to 5 hours (partly covering the pot by putting the lid half on will ensure the liquid reduces to give the stock a more concentrated flavour).

When it's ready, strain into a clean pan and leave to cool. When the stock is quite cold you can then remove the layer of fat that will have formed on the top (and keep this for dripping). The stock is now ready for use: the bones can either be discarded or topped up with more water. This is a basic brown beef stock—for a light stock, use all veal bones instead of beef and dispense with the browning in the oven.

Goulash Soup with Dumplings (Serves 4–6)

1 lb (450 g) shin of beef
2 tablespoons beef dripping
1 large onion, peeled and chopped
2 tablespoons plain flour
1 tablespoon Hungarian paprika
$\frac{1}{4}$ teaspoon dried marjoram
$\frac{1}{2}$ teaspoon caraway seeds
1 clove garlic, crushed
A 14-oz (400-g) tin tomatoes
1$\frac{1}{2}$ pints (850 ml) beef stock
1 teaspoon tomato purée
1 lb (450 g) potatoes, peeled and cut into cubes
1 green pepper, de-seeded and chopped
$\frac{1}{4}$ pint (150 ml) soured cream or yoghurt
Salt and freshly milled black pepper

For the dumplings:
4 oz (110 g) self-raising flour
2 oz (50 g) shredded suet
Salt and freshly milled black pepper

Trim and cut the meat into very small pieces, then heat the beef dripping in a large pan and fry the meat over a high heat until well browned. Now lower the heat a little, stir in the onion and cook until it's lightly browned. Sprinkle in the flour, paprika, marjoram, caraway seeds and garlic. Stir well and cook for a minute or two before adding the tomatoes and stock. When it comes to simmering point, cover and continue simmering very gently for 45 minutes. After that, take the lid off and stir in the tomato purée, followed by the potatoes and chopped pepper, and simmer gently for 10 minutes, stirring occasionally. Then in a bowl, mix the flour and shredded suet, season with salt and pepper, and add enough cold water to make a smooth elastic dough. Divide the dough into 12 small dumplings, pop them on to the soup—don't press them down, though, just let them float. Then put the lid back on and simmer for a further 25 minutes. Taste to check the seasoning and add a dollop of soured cream or yoghurt to each serving.

Split Pea and Vegetable Soup   (Serves 6)

Yellow or green split peas will do for this deliciously thick and substantial soup.

½ lb (225 g) green split peas, washed
3 oz (75 g) butter or bacon fat
4 oz (110 g) streaky bacon, rinded and chopped small
1 medium onion, peeled and chopped
2 sticks celery, chopped
1 large carrot, scraped and chopped
½ small turnip, peeled and chopped
½ small swede, peeled and chopped
3 pints (1–7 litres) stock (or water)
Salt and freshly milled black pepper

First, in a large cooking pot, melt the fat, then cook the bacon and onion in it for 5 minutes before adding the rest of the vegetables—give them a good stir round in the butter and let them colour a little at the edges over a fairly low heat. Then pour in the stock and add the washed split peas. Bring everything back to simmering point, skim the surface if there's any scum, then put a lid on and continue to simmer very gently for about 1½ hours, or until the peas are absolutely soft. Now liquidise the soup just a little (or else sieve it)—but it shouldn't be too uniformly smooth. Taste, season, re-heat and serve the soup garnished with some croûtons crisp-fried in bacon fat.

Note: There's no need to soak the split peas, but the length of cooking time may vary 30 minutes or so either way.

Thick Country Soup

(Serves 6–8)

I say thick, because you could stand your spoon up in this one!
If you prefer it a little thinner, just add more liquid, to your
taste.

½ lb (225 g) dried haricot beans
2 tablespoons oil
1 onion, peeled and chopped
2 cloves garlic, crushed
2 sticks celery, chopped
2 carrots, scraped and chopped
4 oz (110 g) streaky bacon, rinded and chopped
2 leeks, cleaned thoroughly, trimmed, halved lengthways and
    sliced into ¼-inch (5-mm) rings
3 courgettes, unpeeled but trimmed each end and chopped
½ small head Savoy cabbage, shredded
2 teaspoons dried basil
4 tablespoons tomato purée
4 oz (110 g) long-grain rice
Salt and freshly milled black pepper

First, put the beans into a saucepan with 3 pints (1.7 litres) of
cold water, bring to the boil and boil for 2–3 minutes. Then
turn the heat off, put a lid on and leave on one side for about
an hour, to soak. Towards the end of that time, heat the oil in a
large pan and gently fry the onion, garlic, celery, carrots and
bacon together for about 10–15 minutes. Now return to the
soaked beans and bring them back to the boil with the lid on
and simmer for about 30 minutes, or until the beans are
tender. Then, using a draining spoon, scoop out about half
the beans and transfer them to an electric blender. Measure
and add a pint (570 ml) of their cooking water and blend until
smooth; then pour this on to the softened vegetables and add
the remaining whole beans and their cooking water together
with the prepared leeks, courgettes, cabbage, basil and a
further pint (570 ml) of water. Bring it all to the boil, add
the tomato purée and sprinkle in the rice. Stir well, then cover
and simmer very gently for 30 minutes. Finally, taste and
season well with salt and freshly milled pepper.

German Soup with Frankfurters (Serves 4–6)

This soup is made more substantial by the addition of bacon and frankfurters.

2 pints (1.2 litres) stock—preferably homemade
2 medium potatoes, peeled and diced
4 leeks
$\frac{1}{2}$ lb (225 g) turnips
$\frac{1}{2}$ lb (225 g) carrots
1 stick celery
4 oz (110 g) streaky bacon, rinded and chopped
4 long frankfurters (or 6 small)
Salt and freshly milled black pepper

Pour the stock into a largish saucepan with the diced potatoes and bring to the boil; then cover and simmer gently until the potatoes are soft—that should be in about 10 minutes. While that is happening, start to prepare the vegetables: first the leeks, which should be slit open lengthways and then cut across in $\frac{1}{4}$-inch (5-mm) slices. Wash them in several changes of water to get rid of the dust, then drain in a colander. Now take a sharp knife and peel and dice the root vegetables into quite small pieces, and cut up the celery too. The chopped bacon should be fried without any additional fat until it's fairly crisp. Then, as soon as the potato is soft, rub it through a sieve (or liquidise it) and return it to the saucepan together with the vegetables, bacon and any fat that came out of it. Now bring the soup up to a gentle simmer, taste and add some seasoning, then cover and cook gently for about an hour. The frankfurters should be sliced thinly and stirred into the soup to heat through gently just a few minutes before you serve it. Then serve it very hot.

Soupe Les Halles

2 tablespoons butter
2 tablespoons oil
1½ lb (700 g) onions, peeled and thinly sliced
2 cloves garlic, crushed
½ teaspoon granulated sugar
2½ pints (1.5 litres) good beef stock
6 slices French bread (baked till crisp for about 20 minutes in a
    medium oven)
Extra butter
8 oz (225 g) Cheddar or Lancashire cheese, grated
Salt and freshly milled black pepper

Heat the butter and oil together in a large saucepan. Stir in the
sliced onions, garlic and sugar, and cook over a fairly low heat
for about 30 minutes, or until the base of the pan is covered
with a nutty brown, caramelised film (this browning process is
important as it improves the colour of the resulting soup and
also helps considerably with the flavour). Now pour on the
stock, bring the soup to the boil, cover and simmer gently for
about an hour. Then taste the soup and season with salt and
freshly milled black pepper, and pre-heat the grill. Now spread
the slices of baked French bread with butter. Place each slice
in a fireproof soup bowl, ladle the soup on top, and when the
bread surfaces sprinkle grated cheese over the top of each
bowl. Now place the bowls under a hot grill until the cheese is
browned and bubbling.

Potage Flamande (Serves 4–6)

This is nicest made with young Brussels sprouts in November—hopefully after a good frost.

¾ lb (350 g) potatoes
2 leeks
¾ lb (350 g) Brussels sprouts
2 oz (50 g) butter
¾ pint (420 ml) stock
1 pint (570 ml) milk
2 tablespoons top of the milk
Salt and freshly milled black pepper
A squeeze of lemon juice
4 rashers streaky bacon, rinded and grilled

Peel and slice the potatoes first; then halve the leeks lengthways, slice them across fairly thickly and wash and drain them thoroughly. Then trim the bases of the sprouts and discard any damaged outer leaves. Now quarter the larger sprouts and halve the smaller ones. Next melt the butter in a good large saucepan. Add the potatoes, leeks and sprouts, and stir well to coat them nicely in the butter. Cover and cook gently for 5 minutes, then add the stock and milk. Bring to simmering point, cover and cook *very* gently for 20–25 minutes, or until the potatoes are soft. Now liquidise or sieve the soup and return it to the pan; add the top of the milk, then re-heat the soup gently, taste and season with salt and freshly milled pepper, and add a squeeze of lemon juice. The bacon should be grilled until absolutely crisp, then crumbled into the soup before serving.

Note: Instead of the top of the milk and lemon juice, you could add ¼ pint (150 ml) of soured cream—depending on your budget at the time!

Potage Paysanne

(Serves 4–6)

I often make this with the stock left over from boiling a bacon joint.

$\frac{1}{4}$ medium turnip, peeled
$\frac{1}{2}$ small swede, peeled
2 carrots, scraped
2 sticks celery
2 medium onions, peeled
1 large or 2 small leeks, trimmed and washed
A good handful of green Brussels tops (or the inner leaves of a green cabbage)
2–3 oz (50–75 g) dripping (preferably bacon fat)
1 clove garlic, crushed
1–2 pints (570 ml–1.2 litres) stock (or half stock, half water)
2 teaspoons tomato purée
Salt and freshly milled black pepper

First take a chopping board and a sharp knife and peel and chop all the vegetables very finely—the soup is not going to be sieved, so it's important that the vegetables are cut very small. Now take a large cooking pot, melt the fat and stir in all the chopped vegetables except the Brussels tops. Stir them round and round to get a good coating of fat, then add the garlic, put a lid on and let them sweat over a low heat for about 15 minutes—don't worry if they turn a little golden round the edges, but *do* stir them now and then to prevent them sticking. After that, pour in the stock and add the tomato purée. Cover again and simmer gently for 45 minutes, then add the shredded greens. Taste and season with salt and freshly milled pepper, and cook for a further 10 minutes, this time without a lid.

Cream of Celery Soup   (Serves 4–6)

I think this is a delicious soup—best made with English celery after a good November frost.

¾ lb (350 g) sticks celery, trimmed (save the leaves)
1 oz (25 g) butter
¼ lb (110 g) potatoes, peeled and cut into chunks
2 medium leeks (white parts only), sliced and washed
1 pint (570 ml) chicken stock
½ pint (275 ml) milk
¼ teaspoon celery seeds
Salt and freshly milled black pepper
2 tablespoons cream

Melt the butter in a large pan over a low heat. Chop the celery and add it to the pan, together with the potatoes and drained leeks. Then stir to coat the vegetables with butter, cover and cook very gently for about 15 minutes, shaking the pan from time to time to prevent the vegetables from sticking. Next pour in the stock and milk, and sprinkle in the celery seeds and some salt. Bring to simmering point, then cover and cook over a very low heat (watching it doesn't boil over) for 20–25 minutes, or until the vegetables are absolutely tender. Then liquidise or sieve the soup, return the purée to the pan and add the cream. Bring back to the boil, taste, add salt and freshly milled pepper, then just before serving chop up any reserved celery leaves and stir them into the soup.

Carrot and Leek Soup   (Serves 4 as a main course)

This makes a nice change from the more usual Leek and Potato Soup, provided of course the carrots are not too expensive.

1 lb (450 g) leeks
1 lb (450 g) carrots
1 medium onion
1 oz (25 g) dripping
1 clove garlic, crushed
2½ pints (1.5 litres) stock
Salt and freshly milled black pepper
A dash of Worcestershire sauce

First of all prepare the vegetables. The leeks should be trimmed, leaving as much green as possible, then halved lengthways, chopped and washed in plenty of cold water. Then scoop them into a colander to drain. Next peel the carrots and cut them into smallish pieces—and the same goes for the onion. Now take a large saucepan, heat the dripping and add all the prepared vegetables along with the crushed clove of garlic. Stir them around a bit, then cover and 'sweat' them for 10 minutes over a low heat, shaking the pan from time to time. Next pour in the stock, add some seasoning, bring to simmering point, cover and simmer very gently for about 10 minutes, or until the pieces of carrot are tender. Now either sieve or liquidise the soup, then return it to the pan, taste to check the seasoning, add a few drops of Worcestershire sauce and re-heat gently. If you happen to have some Parmesan cheese handy, a little would be very nice sprinkled on each serving.

Potato Soup with Bacon   (Serves 4)

This is a thick, very warming soup, just right when the weather is cold.

1 lb (450 g) potatoes, peeled and chopped
2 large carrots, scraped and chopped
2 sticks celery, chopped
1 small turnip, peeled and chopped
1 medium onion, peeled and chopped
2 oz (50 g) butter or dripping
2 pints (1.2 litres) stock
½ teaspoon dried marjoram
Salt and freshly milled black pepper
2 rashers streaky bacon, rinded

Take a large thick-based saucepan and melt the butter or dripping over a very gentle heat. Then add all the prepared vegetables, stirring them around to get them well coated with the fat. Cover with a well-fitting lid, and with the heat kept very low let the vegetables 'sweat' gently for about 15 minutes—if you give the pan a shake from time to time you won't have any trouble with the vegetables sticking. After 15 minutes pour in the stock and add the marjoram and some salt and pepper. Then put the lid almost back on but leave a ½-inch (1-cm) gap at the edge (to let some of the steam escape). Simmer the soup like this for about another 20 minutes, or until the vegetables are soft.

Now you can either sieve or liquidise half the contents of the saucepan, and then return them to the other half. This means that the soup will be thickened nicely and will still have some bits of vegetable in it for texture. Next, grill or fry the bacon rashers until crisp, and crumble them into the soup in little bits. I think this soup is nice served with some croûtons crisp-fried in bacon fat.

Cauliflower Soup   (Serves 4 as a main course)

As cauliflowers are available all the year round and prices tend to fluctuate enormously, this soup is only really economical when the price is right.

1 largish cauliflower
1 pint (570 ml) stock (a light chicken stock or just plain water)
1 bayleaf
1 pint (570 ml) milk
¾ lb (350 g) potatoes, peeled and chopped small
A squeeze of lemon juice
Freshly grated nutmeg
Salt and freshly milled black pepper
1 tablespoon cream, top of the milk or soured cream
  (whatever's available)

First separate the florets of the cauliflower from the hard stalk (this can be kept and grated for a salad). Now you need to separate the florets themselves into very tiny pieces. Then in a medium saucepan bring the stock and bayleaf to simmering point, throw in the little pieces of cauliflower and simmer them for about 6 minutes, or until they are just cooked but still have some 'bite'. Lift them out with a draining spoon and keep them on one side. Pour in the milk now and add the potatoes, then simmer gently without a lid until the potatoes are soft— about 10 minutes. Next rub the soup through a sieve, or liquidise it, and return it to the saucepan. Now return the cauliflower to the saucepan and re-heat gently, adding a squeeze of lemon juice. Some salt and pepper, and a scraping of nutmeg. Then stir in the cream just before serving.

Soupe au Chou (Serves 4–6)

The reason this has a French title is because, as well as being French inspired, 'Soupe au Chou' sounds more promising than 'Bacon and Cabbage Soup'.

$\frac{1}{2}$ white cabbage
1 oz (25 g) dripping or bacon fat
$\frac{1}{2}$ lb (225 g) unsmoked streaky bacon, rinded and diced
2 medium onions, peeled and chopped
1 medium potato, peeled and chopped
1 leek, sliced and washed
1 clove garlic, crushed
3 pints (1.7 litres) stock
Salt and freshly milled black pepper
Freshly grated nutmeg

Prepare the cabbage by first cutting out any hard stalky bits or ribs and then shredding the leaves as thinly as possible. Now blanch the cabbage by placing it in a saucepan of cold water, bringing it to the boil and boiling for 1 minute, after which it needs to be drained in a colander. Now, using the same saucepan, heat the fat and fry the bacon until the fat starts to run from it. Then add the onion, potato, leek and garlic, stir all the vegetables around, and cook them until softened and slightly golden. Next stir in the drained cabbage and cook for another minute or two before pouring in the stock. Bring it back to the boil and then simmer it very gently without a lid for about an hour. Finally taste and season with salt and pepper and a little freshly grated nutmeg.

EGGS AND US

Well actually the egg and I are great companions. I love them pure and simple, as the advert says—in fact, I'm almost obsessed with them, forever stopping the car on country roads and peeping over fences where the sign says 'Eggs For Sale' just to see if the hens are running about, as my grandmother puts it.

Alas, free-range is unrealistic nowadays, so mostly I make do with the supermarket variety. Mind you, I'm just as obsessive there too—because *fresh* certainly isn't unrealistic and I'll always be grateful to the EEC for introducing packing date-stamps on egg boxes. I no longer have to gaze and wonder how long they've been hanging about: it tells you. I suppose, if you're in a hurry, it *can* take a while to tot up which Week 34 is—but persevere, because if we have to eat battery eggs, then at least they must be fresh.

Once you have a few fresh eggs in the house you'll never be short of a quick cheap meal: there's something very reassuring about lightly boiled eggs served with 'soldiers' of brown bread and butter, and freshly made tea. However, in this chapter we're after something different—still the same good old standby eggs but made into main meals that won't cost much extra (but *taste* as if they did!).

Curried Egg Patties (Serves 2)

This is good for an unexpected meal, provided you have half a dozen eggs in the house.

4 hardboiled eggs, chopped small
2 oz (50 g) butter
1½ oz (40 g) plain flour
1 teaspoon Madras curry powder
1 teaspoon salt
¼ pint (150 ml) milk
1 egg, beaten
1 teaspoon tomato purée
½ teaspoon Worcestershire sauce
½ teaspoon lemon juice

To coat and cook:
Seasoned plain flour
1 egg, beaten
Dried breadcrumbs
Oil for frying

Melt the butter in a saucepan, then stir in the flour, curry powder and salt. Cook for 2 minutes, then gradually stir in the milk to make a very thick sauce. Cook this for 5 minutes, stirring all the time, and then take the pan off the heat and add the beaten egg, tomato purée, Worcestershire sauce and lemon juice. Now add the hardboiled eggs, stir to mix them in, then season with salt. Next transfer the mixture to a bowl, cover and chill until the mixture becomes firm. Then before cooking form the mixture into 4 little round cakes, about ¾ inch (2 cm) thick, and dip them first in the seasoned flour, then in the beaten egg and finally in the breadcrumbs. Now shallow-fry them in ¼ inch (5 mm) of hot oil till golden brown and drain on kitchen paper before serving.

Poached Eggs with Soufflé'd Welsh Rarebit

4 fresh eggs for poaching
$\frac{1}{2}$ oz (10 g) butter
$\frac{1}{2}$ oz (10 g) flour
6 tablespoons milk
$\frac{1}{2}$ teaspoon French mustard
A dash of Worcestershire sauce
A little cayenne pepper
2 extra eggs, separated
1 oz (25 g) strong Cheddar cheese, grated
1 oz (25 g) Parmesan, grated
4 slices white bread (medium thick)
Salt and freshly milled black pepper

First heat some water in a frying pan with a little salt ready to poach the eggs in. Then take a small saucepan, melt the butter in it, stir in the flour and cook over a medium heat for a minute or two before gradually stirring in the milk. Allow the mixture to bubble for 2 minutes, then take the saucepan off the heat and stir in the seasonings. Now beat the yolks of the two extra separated eggs; then stir the yolks into the sauce and leave the mixture until it's cold. Next beat in the grated cheeses. Whisk the egg whites until stiff and carefully fold them into the cheese mixture. Now toast the bread on both sides and cover each slice thickly with the cheese mixture. Cook under a medium grill until the cheese mixture is puffed up and dark brown on top. During the last part—whilst you grill the cheese mixture—slip the 4 eggs into simmering water to poach for 3 minutes. Lift them out with a draining spoon, resting it on kitchen paper to drain each egg, then pop one on each of the toasts.

Eggs with Cheese and Spinach Sauce

(Serves 2)

This is very colourful to look at and quite filling served with rice and a green salad.

½ lb (225 g) fresh spinach leaves, cooked and drained, or ¼ lb
  (110 g) frozen spinach (thawed)
4 large eggs
1 small onion, peeled and finely chopped
2 oz (50 g) butter
1 oz (25 g) plain flour
½ pint (275 ml) milk
3 oz (75 g) Cheddar cheese, grated
2 tablespoons cream
Salt and freshly milled pepper
Freshly grated nutmeg

Melt 1½ oz (40 g) of the butter in a small saucepan and gently soften the onion in it for 10 minutes. Then stir in the flour, cook for a minute or two and add the milk a little at a time, stirring after each addition, to make a smooth sauce. Taste and season the sauce, and let it cook for 6 minutes over a very gently heat. Meanwhile boil the eggs by placing them in cold water, bringing them up to the boil and simmering them for 6 minutes, afterwards cooling them under cold running water. Now add two-thirds of the grated cheese to the sauce, stir it in and allow it to melt; then transfer the sauce to a liquidiser, add the remaining ½ oz (10 g) butter, the cream and the chopped drained spinach, and whizz the sauce until it's a pale green colour and only very tiny speckles of the spinach are visible. Season the sauce again, adding some nutmeg. Peel the eggs now, then halve them. Put a layer of sauce in a buttered gratin dish and arrange the eggs on top, rounded side up. Cover with the rest of the sauce, sprinkle with the remainder of the grated cheese and place the dish under a hot grill until the cheese is brown and the sauce is bubbling.

Egg and Bacon Pie

(Serves 4)

I've always found the conventional egg and bacon pie a bit on the dry side: however, try it this way, you'll find it's a whole lot nicer.

For the filling:
4 large eggs
6 rashers lean streaky bacon, rinded
Salt and freshly milled black pepper
$\frac{1}{4}$ pint (150 ml) milk

For the shortcrust pastry:
6 oz (175 g) plain flour
3 oz (75 g) lard
A pinch each salt and pepper
Cold water to mix

Pre-heat the oven to mark 6/400°F/200°C with a baking sheet in it

First hardboil 3 of the eggs by placing them in a saucepan, covering them with cold water, bringing it up to the boil and simmering gently for 7 minutes; then cool them rapidly under cold running water. Next either grill or fry the bacon rashers gently until the fat starts to run. While they're cooking, and the eggs are cooling, make the pastry (see page 212). Divide it in half, and use half to line a 7-inch (18 cm) flan tin (if possible one with a $1\frac{1}{2}$-inch (4cm) deep rim with sloping sides). Now peel and chop the hardboiled eggs quite small, and chop the bacon fairly small as well. Next arrange the chopped bacon and eggs in the flan and season with freshly milled pepper and only a very little salt—because of the bacon. Now beat the remaining egg with the milk and pour it over the contents of the pie. Then roll out the rest of the pastry to make a lid, dampen the edges and seal well. Decorate with any trimmings, make a small hole in the centre and brush the top with milk. Place the pie on the baking sheet on a highish shelf in the oven and bake for 10 minutes; then reduce the heat to mark 4/350°F/180°C and bake for a further 30 minutes. This pie is very good eaten cold and is ideal picnic food.

Cheese Soufflé   (Serves 3–4)

This is always a good standby recipe for using up old bits of cheese that lurk in the bottom of the fridge.

3 oz (75 g) cheese, grated
3 large eggs, separated
1 oz (25 g) plain flour
1 oz (25 g) butter
¼ pint (150 ml) milk
2 pinches cayenne pepper
½ teaspoon mustard powder
A few gratings nutmeg
Salt and freshly milled black pepper
A little extra butter

Pre-heat the oven to mark 5/375°F/190°C

Well butter a 1½-pint (850 ml) soufflé dish. Then take a medium-sized saucepan, melt 1 oz (25 g) butter in it, add the flour and stir it over a medium heat for 2 minutes. Now add the milk gradually, stirring all the time till you have a smooth paste, and cook it very gently for 3 minutes (still stirring). Next stir in the mustard, cayenne, nutmeg, salt and pepper, and allow the sauce to cool a bit before stirring in the grated cheese, followed by the egg yolks—which should be beaten quite thoroughly first. Now whisk the egg whites till stiff, beat a couple of dollops into the sauce, then fold the rest in very carefully and gently, so as not to lose all the air you've beaten into them. Pile the mixture into the soufflé dish next, then place it on a baking sheet in the centre of the oven for about 30–35 minutes. To test if the soufflé is cooked, push a skewer down into the centre—if it comes out clean and doesn't look too liquid, it's cooked.

Poached Eggs with Spinach Soufflé

(Serves 4)

A very impressive way to serve eggs and spinach.

2 lb (900 g) fresh spinach
4 fresh eggs
2 oz (50 g) butter
2 oz (50 g) plain flour
$\frac{1}{2}$ pint (275 ml) milk
2 oz (50 g) cheese, grated
3 egg yolks
4 egg whites
Freshly grated nutmeg
Some more butter
Dry white breadcrumbs
Salt and freshly milled black pepper

Pre-heat the oven to mark 5/375°F/190°C with a baking sheet in it

First of all liberally butter a soufflé dish (7 inches/18 cm in diameter) and dust the inside of the dish evenly with a few dry white breadcrumbs. Then thoroughly wash the spinach in several changes of cold water and pick it over, removing any thick, tough stalks or damaged leaves. Next press the leaves into a large saucepan, sprinkle with 2 teaspoons of salt (but don't add water), cover and cook for 7–10 minutes. Then drain the spinach thoroughly in a colander and chop it fairly finely. Now melt 2 oz (50 g) butter in a medium-sized saucepan and stir in the flour. Cook for a minute or two before gradually stirring in the milk. Bring to boiling point and simmer, still stirring, for about 1 minute before removing the pan from the heat. Then beat the chopped spinach and two-thirds of the cheese into the mixture with the egg yolks. Now taste and season with salt, pepper and a generous amount of nutmeg. At this stage *lightly* poach the 4 eggs for 3 minutes in a frying pan of barely simmering water. While they're poaching, beat the egg whites till stiff, fold them carefully into the spinach mixture, then pour half the soufflé mixture into the dish, add the poached eggs (well drained), cover with the rest of the soufflé mixture and sprinkle the top with the remaining cheese. Bake on the baking sheet for 30–35 minutes, or until it is well risen and browned on top.

Cauliflower, Egg and Celery au Gratin

(Serves 3–4)

This is a good one for vegetarians or anyone else who wants a delicious meal without any meat.

1 head English celery
1 cauliflower
2 hardboiled eggs, quartered
¼ lb (110 g) mushrooms, sliced
1 large onion, peeled and chopped
2 oz (50 g) butter
2 oz (50 g) plain flour
½ pint (275 ml) milk
3 oz (75 g) Cheddar cheese, grated
1 tablespoon dried breadcrumbs
1 bayleaf
¼ whole nutmeg, grated
Salt and freshly milled black pepper
2 pinches cayenne pepper
A little extra butter

Pre-heat the oven to mark 7/425°F/220°C

Scrub and chop the celery into chunks and cook it in a little boiling salted water for about 20 minutes. The cauliflower needs to be trimmed, washed and sat in about 1 inch (2.5 cm) of boiling salted water, together with the bayleaf, for about 10–15 minutes with the lid on the saucepan (both the celery and the cauliflower should be tender but still firm). When the cauliflower is ready, drain it—reserving the water—then separate it into small florets and arrange them in a buttered fireproof dish along with the celery, sliced mushrooms and the quarters of hardboiled egg. Now make the sauce by gently cooking the chopped onion in 2 oz (50 g) of butter for about 10 minutes,

43

then stirring in the flour and adding the milk bit by bit, stirring all the time. When all the milk is in, add $\frac{1}{4}-\frac{1}{2}$ pint (150–275 ml) of cauliflower water in the same way till you have a smooth sauce. Cook it gently for 6 minutes, then taste it, add salt and pepper and about $\frac{1}{4}$ of a whole nutmeg, grated. Pour the sauce over the vegetables, sprinkle the grated cheese over, then the bread-crumbs, dot with flecks of butter and bake on a high shelf for 10 minutes until the cheese has browned and melted. Sprinkle with a couple of pinches of cayenne and serve hot.

Egg and Anchovy Salad (Serves 4)

This is a nice dish for lunch on a hot summer's day with, maybe, a cold soup to start with.

6 eggs
1 lb (450g) new potatoes (cooked)
$\frac{1}{4}$ lb (110g) cooked French beans (or sliced runner beans)
Salt and freshly milled black pepper
1 quantity of vinaigrette dressing (see page 143)

To finish
1 lettuce, cleaned and prepared
A 2-oz (60g) tin anchovy fillets, well drained
1 oz (25g) black olives

Put the eggs in a saucepan, cover them with cold water, bring them up to a gentle simmer and cook gently for exactly 7 minutes. Then cool them rapidly under cold running water until they're quite cold. Now take the shells off and chop the eggs roughly, seasoning them with a little salt and pepper. Then slice the potatoes into rounds and cut the beans into 1-inch (2.5-cm) lengths. Now take a large bowl, carefully mix the chopped eggs, beans and potatoes together, and pour in nearly all the vinaigrette dressing, keeping a little for later. Stir again, to get everything coated with the dressing, then cover the mixture and chill it until needed. To serve the salad, arrange the lettuce leaves in a salad bowl and sprinkle them with the reserved dressing; then arrange the potato mixture over the lettuce, make a criss-cross pattern with the anchovies and finally sprinkle on the black olives.

Potato and Cheese Baked Eggs   (Serves 2)

This is a fairly economical supper dish that tastes especially good with homemade tomato sauce.

4 large fresh eggs
A little extra butter
4 large fresh eggs
2 lb (900g) potatoes
Salt and freshly milled black pepper
3 oz (75 g) butter
A 5-floz (150-ml) carton soured cream
6 oz (175g) Cheddar cheese, grated
A few chopped chives or spring onion tops

Pre-heat the oven to mark 5/375°F/190°C

Peel the potatoes, place them in a saucepan with some salt, pour boiling water on to them and cook them for about 25 minutes, or until tender. Then drain them, add 3 oz (75g) of the butter and the soured cream, start to mash them with a fork and finish off by whipping them to a purée with an electric mixer. Now add the cheese, taste and season with salt and pepper. Next butter a shallow ovenproof baking dish, arrange the potato mixture in the dish and, with the back of a tablespoon, make 4 depressions. Now break an egg carefully into each depression, place the dish in the oven and bake for 15 minutes, or until the eggs are just set. Serve sprinkled with chopped chives or spring onion tops.

Eggs Savoyard

(Serves 4)

For this recipe for 4 people you could use 4 individual oven-proof bowls (about ½ pint/275ml capacity), but failing that you can cook the whole lot in a large gratin dish.

1 lb (450g) potatoes, peeled
2 oz (50g) butter
1 onion, peeled and finely chopped
4 eggs
8 tablespoons single cream
4 oz (110g) Cheddar cheese, grated
Salt and freshly milled black pepper

Pre-heat the oven to mark 6/400°F/200°C

First of all place the potatoes in a saucepan with some salt, pour in some boiling water and cook them for about 25 minutes. Then drain them, slice the potatoes (as you would for frying) and arrange an equal quantity in the base of each bowl. Next heat the butter in a saucepan and fry the onion until softened and golden. Then spoon a little of the melted butter and onion mixture over the sliced potatoes in each dish, and season with freshly milled pepper and salt. Now make a slight depression in each bowl and carefully break in an egg. Next spoon 2 tablespoons of cream over each egg and season again with salt and pepper. Then sprinkle with cheese and bake in the oven for 15–20 minutes, or until hot and bubbling with the yolk still fairly soft. Serve absolutely immediately.

Bacon, Leek and Potato Omelette

(Serves 2)

This is a flat omelette, finished off under the grill, so it shouldn't be folded—just simply cut in half or in quarters.

4 large eggs
2 potatoes
1 leek
2 tablespoons oil
4 oz (110g) streaky bacon, rinded and diced
Salt and freshly milled black pepper
A generous pinch mixed herbs

Peel and dice the potatoes and dry them on some kitchen paper; then trim the leek top and bottom. Slice it in half first lengthways and then across into ¼-inch (5-mm) thick strips, wash carefully in plenty of cold water, and drain and dry thoroughly. In a frying pan, about 6 inches (15cm) in diameter, heat the oil and add the diced potato. Cook gently for about 10 minutes, stirring frequently. When the potato is just tender, add the chopped leek and diced bacon to the pan. Stir well, cover with a suitably sized lid and cook over a low heat for a further 5–8 minutes. Meanwhile break the eggs into a bowl. Season well with salt, freshly milled pepper and mixed herbs. Stir to blend the eggs together, then pour the mixture over the contents of the pan. Shake the pan and cook over a low heat until the underside of the omelette is cooked and lightly golden. Meanwhile pre-heat the grill, then transfer the pan to the grill and continue to cook gently until the egg on the surface is just set. Cut the omelette in half or quarters and serve on warmed plates. This is nice with a crisp salad.

Spanish Tortilla

(Serves 2)

Tortilla, or Spanish omelette, can sometimes be just a mish-mash of leftovers incorporated in an omelette—but this is a real one made with green peppers and Spanish chorizo sausage.

4 large eggs
3 tablespoons oil
2 potatoes, peeled and diced
1 medium onion, peeled and chopped
1 small green pepper, de-seeded and chopped
A 2-oz (50-g) piece Spanish chorizo sausage, also chopped
  small
Salt and freshly milled black pepper

For this you need a thick, heavy, medium-sized frying pan. Put 2 tablespoons of oil in it, then add the diced potatoes and cook them gently for about 8–10 minutes, stirring them around so that they brown evenly. Next add the onion, pepper and chorizo, stir again and continue cooking for a further 8–10 minutes, or until the potato and onion are soft. Now break the eggs into a bowl, season them well, beat them just a little bit with a fork, then pour them into the pan and, keeping the heat at medium, cook for 2 or 3 minutes, shaking the pan from time to time to prevent the eggs from sticking. When the omelette is firm but still slightly moist, slide it out on to a plate, then quickly heat the other tablespoon of oil in the pan and slide the omelette back in on its other side. Cook for another 3 minutes and serve cut in wedges.

Omelette Piperade

(Serves 2)

Another quick supper dish for 2 people; good towards the end of the summer when the tomatoes are plentiful and green peppers are cheap.

For 2 omelettes the ingredients are:

4 eggs
Oil or butter
1 large green pepper, de-seeded and chopped
1 onion, peeled and chopped
1 clove garlic, crushed
$\frac{1}{2}$ lb (225 g) ripe tomatoes, skinned and chopped
$\frac{1}{2}$ teaspoon dried basil
Salt and freshly milled black pepper

Heat a little oil in a medium-sized pan, then stir in the chopped pepper, chopped onion and crushed garlic, and cook over a medium heat for about 5 minutes. Then add the tomatoes and dried basil, season with salt and freshly milled black pepper, and cook gently without a cover for about 20 minutes. Now get ready for the first omelette by breaking 2 eggs into a bowl, seasoning with salt and pepper and stirring lightly with a fork. Then heat a smear of oil in an omelette pan and, when it is really hot, pour in the beaten egg and start to draw the eggs in to cook the omelette. After a few seconds, spoon half the pepper and tomato mixture over half the omelette, fold the other half of the omelette over the filling and invert the pan to tip the omelette out on to a warmed plate. Now quickly prepare the other omelette, using the remaining filling, and serve immediately with some crusty bread and a nice crisp green salad.

Frugal Fish

The funny thing is, frugal fish is usually the freshest. The more expensive deep-sea fish, like cod and haddock, are very often three weeks old before they're landed—and (in my opinion) their dull flavour shows it. Since our home-caught herring and mackerel have far more character and flavour, I wonder why it's necessary to go off and fight wars over dull old cod?

But then we are a nation of fish-finger addicts, and once you're bitten your way through the bright orange bread-crumbs, what you've got is probably cod. We've already spoken of convenience versus cost but, quite honestly, fish fingers are outrageously expensive (I once reckoned up the price per pound of frozen fish fingers and discovered that in the same supermarket frozen rainbow trout was actually cheaper, and as it happens every bit as convenient but without the nasty breadcrumbs).

In this chapter I'm hoping to lure you on to a few very delicious recipes for herring and mackerel. I think it's a pity that because they were once less than a halfpenny each they've always had a poverty-stricken reputation. Well, when it comes to shopping for food we're all pretty poor now, so here's to their comeback! In the other recipes in this chapter I've attempted to make a little fish go a long way.

Also, when a recipe calls for white fish, do try the lesser-known varieties like pollack or red fish (sometimes called Norwegian cod) which are usually half the price of cod or haddock—and for any sort of fish pie, coley is very good.

Whiting au Gratin   (Serves 4)

2 lb (900 g) whiting (ask the fishmonger to fillet and skin it for
  you)
1 oz (25 g) butter
1 onion, peeled, halved and thinly sliced
4 oz (110 g) mushrooms, thinly sliced
1 teaspoon lemon juice
 Salt and freshly milled black pepper
3 fl (75 ml) oz dry cider
4 tablespoons dry white breadcrumbs
2 tablespoons grated cheese
A little extra butter

Pre-heat the oven to mark 4/350°F/180°C

First heat 1oz (25 g) of butter in a saucepan and fry the onion
gently until softened (about 10 minutes). Then stir in the
mushrooms and lemon juice, and cook for about 3–4 minutes
more. Season with salt and pepper, then spread the mixture
over the base of a buttered gratin dish. Lay the wiped fillets on
top and season again with salt and pepper. Next pour in just
enough cider to cover the mushroom/onion base. Finally
sprinkle the breadcrumbs and cheese all over, dot with flecks
of butter and bake—uncovered—on a high shelf in the oven
for 25 minutes.

Old-fashioned Soused Herrings

(Serves 3)

Homemade rollmops beat anything that ever came out of a jar.

6 herrings
6 teaspoons made mustard
2 dill pickles, sliced lengthways into 3
1 large onion, peeled and thinly sliced into rings
$\frac{1}{2}$ pint (275 ml) cider vinegar
$\frac{1}{4}$ pint (150 ml) dry cider
$\frac{3}{4}$ pint (420 ml) water
3 juniper berries
3 allspice berries
2 cloves
8 peppercorns
1 bayleaf

Pre-heat the oven to mark 4/350°F/180°C

You will need a shallow baking dish or casserole for this and also 6 toothpicks.

Ask the fishmonger to head, gut and fillet the herrings but to leave their tails on. When you get them home, check that all the bones have been removed and wipe the fillets as dry as possible with some kitchen paper. Now spread the filleted side of each fish with a teaspoon of mustard and place a slice of dill pickle across what was the head end of each fillet. Sprinkle the rest with some of the separated onion rings, roll up each fillet from the head end to the tail, being careful to get them as tight and neat as possible, and secure with a toothpick (through the tail end and out the other side). Now pack the rolls fairly tightly into the baking dish or casserole. Then prepare the marinade by placing the vinegar, cider and water in a sauce-pan, together with the spices and bayleaf. Bring the liquid to the boil and simmer (uncovered) for 10 minutes. Then take the pan from the heat and leave until the liquid is cold. To cook the herrings, pour the cold marinade over, cover with a lid or double foil and bake in the centre of the oven for 15 minutes. When they're cooked, let them get quite cold in the liquid, then cover them and put them in the refrigerator for at least 48 hours before serving. Serve, if possible, with rye bread.

Herrings Fried in Oatmeal (Serves 2)

Just the thing for 'high tea' with some brown bread and butter and freshly made tea.

4 herrings, gutted
2 oz (50 g) lard
3 tablespoons medium oatmeal
Salt and freshly milled black pepper

First gut the herrings as described on page 54. Then heat the lard in a large frying pan and, while it's heating, wipe the herrings with kitchen paper to get them as dry as possible. Season the oatmeal with freshly milled black pepper and salt, and then coat the herrings in it, pressing it down all over quite firmly. When the fat is hot and sizzling, fry the herrings in it for approximately 4 minutes on each side, until they're crisp and golden. Then drain them on crumpled greaseproof paper and serve with wedges of lemon to squeeze over them. Powdered mustard mixed with cream (or top of the milk) goes very well with this dish and, instead of bread and butter, plain boiled potatoes.

Baked Fish Soufflé

(Serves 4)

12 ounces (350g) of whiting fillets, or any white fish, is instantly made more special by making it into a fluffy soufflé.

12 oz (350g) whiting fillets (cooked in ½ pint/275 ml of milk
  then strained—with the milk reserved)
2 oz (50 g) butter
1½ oz (40g) plain flour
4 egg yolks
2 tablespoons grated Parmesan
2 teaspoons lemon juice
1 tablespoon finely chopped parsley
1 teaspoon anchovy essence
3 spring onions, finely sliced
5 egg whites
Salt and cayenne pepper

Pre-heat the oven to mark 6/400°F/200°C

Flake the fish, discarding the skin and bones as you go, then put it on one side whilst you make a sauce by melting the butter in a saucepan then stirring in the flour. Cook this for a minute or two before gradually adding the strained milk. Bring to the boil, stirring, and boil gently for 1 minute. Then remove the pan from the heat and beat in the egg yolks, 1 tablespoon of Parmesan, the lemon juice, parsley, anchovy essence, spring onion and the fish. Season well with salt and ½ teaspoon of cayenne pepper. Next whisk the egg whites to the stiff peak stage. Then fold them into the fish mixture, taste and season again if necessary. Now pour the mixture into a buttered 3-pint (1.75-litre) soufflé dish or deep baking dish, and sprinkle with the remaining Parmesan cheese. Transfer the soufflé to the oven, placing it on a baking sheet, and turn down the heat immediately to mark 5/375°F/190°C. Cook for 35–40 minutes, or until the soufflé is well risen and golden brown, then serve absolutely immediately.

56

Baked Fish with Potatoes and Anchovies

(Serves 3)

Any white fish can be used for this, because there's lots of flavour added.

1 lb (450 g) potatoes, peeled and very thinly sliced
1 lb (450 g) white fish, skinned
1 oz (25 g) butter
1 onion, peeled and finely chopped
6 tablespoons chopped parsley
1 clove garlic, crushed
Finely grated rind of 1 lemon
6 anchovy fillets, finely chopped
$\frac{1}{4}$ pint (150 ml) milk
Salt and freshly milled black pepper

Pre-heat the oven to mark 4/350°F/180°C

Put a layer of potato slices in the base of a deepish, well-buttered baking dish and sprinkle with half the finely chopped onion. Then mix the parsley, garlic, lemon rind and finely chopped anchovy fillets together and sprinkle a little of this mixture in the dish before adding another layer of potatoes, some onion and another sprinkling of parsley mixture. Finish off with a final layer of potatoes (reserving a little of the parsley mixture). Now bring the milk up to the boil, season with a little salt and plenty of pepper, then pour this over the potatoes, fleck the top with butter and bake (uncovered) for 40 minutes. Meanwhile cut the fish into smallish cubes; then after the 40 minutes is up, put the fish on top of the potatoes and sprinkle with the remaining parsley mixture and a few more flecks of butter, and bake for a further 15 minutes, or until the fish is cooked.

Mackerel en Papillote

Cooking mackerel in paper cases keeps the flesh beautifully moist and tender.

2 mackerel, headed and gutted
2 oz (50 g) butter
4 tablespoons finely chopped parsley
1 small onion, peeled and grated
1 clove garlic, crushed
Juice of 1 lemon
$\frac{1}{4}$ teaspoon dried tarragon
A generous pinch cayenne pepper
$1\frac{1}{2}$ oz (40 g) butter, melted
Salt and freshly milled black pepper

Pre-heat the oven to mark 6/400°F/200°C

Wipe the fish as dry as possible with kitchen paper, inside and out, and season them with salt and freshly milled black pepper. Then mix the 2 oz (50 g) of butter with the parsley, onion, garlic, lemon juice, tarragon and cayenne pepper and beat everything thoroughly to blend well. Then spread and equal quantity inside each fish. Now take two large circles of double thickness greaseproof paper (each large enough to take a fish comfortably) and brush them with the melted butter. Then lay each fish in the middle on the buttered side, and wrap one side of the paper circle over the fish (to make a sort of Cornish pasty shape). Secure the edges by pinching them together, making small folds, then pop both parcels on to a baking sheet and bake for 30 minutes. Unwrap and serve with the juice from the packets poured over.

Mackerel with Rhubarb Sauce (Serves 2)

Not quite so famous as mackerel with gooseberries but just as good—the acidic fruit counteracts the richness of the fish perfectly.

2 mackerel, gutted (ask the fishmonger to do this for you)
½ lb (225 g) rhubarb
1 level tablespoon demerara sugar
½ level teaspoon ground ginger
¼ pint (150 ml) water
Salt and freshly milled black pepper

Make the sauce first by chopping the rhubarb into smallish chunks and putting it into a thick-based saucepan, adding the sugar, ginger and water. Then put a lid on and let it cook over a fairly gentle heat, shaking the saucepan from time to time. It will probably take around 15–20 minutes to soften. Now rub the contents of the saucepan through a sieve, or purée it in an electric blender, and taste to check that there is enough sugar (although it should be a fairly sharp sauce). Now pre-heat the grill, wipe the mackerel as dry as possible with kitchen paper, season the insides of the fish, then make three diagonal slashes across the backbone of each fish and grill them for about 4–6 minutes on each side. While they're grilling, re-heat the sauce and serve it with the fish, together with new potatoes.

Fish Cakes with Capers (Serves 4–6)

A good way to make a pound (450 g) of fish seem just like 2 pounds (950 g).

1 lb (450 g) creamed, mashed potatoes
1 lb (450 g) poached cod (well drained)
2 tablespoons chopped parsley
¾ teaspoon anchovy essence
1 heaped teaspoon capers, chopped
1 egg, beaten
1 oz (25 g) butter
1 teaspoon lemon juice
Some grated nutmeg
1 clove garlic, crushed
Salt and freshly milled black pepper
A generous pinch cayenne pepper

For the coating:
Plain flour
2 eggs, beaten
6 oz (175 g) (approx.) dry white breadcrumbs
Oil and butter for frying

Take a large mixing bowl and thoroughly combine all the ingredients (except those for the coating) together; then taste; adding salt and pepper and a pinch of cayenne. (If the fish and potatoes are not freshly cooked and hot, the butter will need to be melted before adding it to the mixture.) Now cool and chill the mixture for an hour or two to get it nice and firm, then when you're ready to cook the fish cakes, lightly flour a working surface, turn the fish mixture out on to it and form it into a long roll about 2–2½ inches (5–6cm) in diameter. Cut the roll into 12 round fish cakes. Pat each cake into a neat shape, and dip each one first into beaten egg and then in the dry white breadcrumbs. Now shallow-fry the cakes in equal quantities of oil and butter until golden brown on both sides. Drain on crumpled kitchen paper and serve immediately. Tartare sauce or fresh parsley sauce would be a nice accompaniment.

Deep-fried Sprats with Mustard Sauce

(Serves 2)

Sprats are smaller cousins belonging to the herring family. In the good old days when herrings were cheap and humble, sprats were even humbler and it's only now that they're coming into their own again, which is a good thing because they are delicious.

1 lb (450 g) sprats
Some seasoned flour
Groundnut oil for frying
2 pinches cayenne pepper

For the mustard sauce:
1 oz (25 g) butter
$\frac{1}{2}$ small onion, peeled and chopped
$\frac{1}{2}$ oz (10 g) flour
2 teaspoons mustard powder
$\frac{1}{2}$ pint (275 ml) milk
Salt and freshly milled black pepper
2 teaspoons lemon juice
A generous pinch sugar

Begin by making the mustard sauce. In a saucepan melt the butter and soften the chopped onion in it for about 10 minutes. Then stir in the flour, and let it cook very gently for a couple of minutes before mixing in the mustard powder. Next add the milk bit by bit, stirring constantly. When all the milk is in, bring the sauce to the boil and let it simmer very gently for about 3 minutes. Then season to taste with salt, freshly milled black pepper, lemon juice and a pinch of sugar. Now keep the sauce warm whilst you gut and cook the sprats.

Make a small incision behind a gill of each fish and gently squeeze the belly up towards the head to gut the fish, at the same time trying to leave the head intact. Then rinse the fish well and dry them thoroughly on some kitchen paper before tossing in seasoned flour. Next heat a deep pan of oil to 350°F/180°C, or, if you don't have a thermometer, until a small cube of bread dropped into it turns golden and crisp in 1 minute. Then fry the sprats in the oil for about 3 minutes. You will probably need to fry them in at least 2 batches. Then drain on crumpled greaseproof paper, keeping them hot, and serve as soon as possible sprinkled with a trace of cayenne and with the mustard sauce poured over.

Herrings with Caper Stuffing (Serves 4)

4 herrings, gutted and boned
1 oz (25 g) butter
For the stuffing:
3 oz (75 g) fresh white breadcrumbs
1 teaspoon mustard powder
3 tablespoons finely chopped parsley
Zest of 1 lemon, finely grated
Juice of ½ lemon
1 tablespoon drained capers, chopped
1 oz (25 g) butter
1 medium onion, peeled and finely chopped
Salt and freshly milled black pepper

Pre-heat the oven to mark 7/425°F/220°C

To make the stuffing, first mix the breadcrumbs, mustard powder, parsley, lemon rind and juice, and capers together in a large mixing bowl. Now heat the butter in a frying pan and soften the onion in it for 10 minutes, before adding it (together with its buttery juices) to the breadcrumbs mixture and seasoning everything with salt and freshly milled pepper.

Now open each herring out flat, and spread a quarter of the stuffing down one side of each one, then fold the other side back to its original shape. Put the fish in a well-buttered shallow baking dish (or else a roasting tin lined with foil), place a knob of butter on each one and bake near the top of the oven for 15 minutes, basting once with the buttery juices.

Kipper Quiche

(Serves 4 as a main course)

A less frugal version of this can be made for a special occasion by substituting $\frac{1}{2}$ pint (275 ml) cream for the milk.

A pair of kippers (about 12 oz/350 g)
6 oz (175 g) shortcrust pastry (see page 212)
A squeeze of lemon juice
$\frac{1}{2}$ pint (275 ml) milk
2 large eggs
2 teaspoons French mustard
Freshly grated nutmeg
Salt and freshly milled black pepper
A generous pinch cayenne pepper

Pre-heat the oven to mark 4/350°F/180°C with a baking sheet in it

Grill the kippers for a few minutes on each side, then set them aside to cool. Meanwhile make the pastry and line a 9–9$\frac{1}{2}$-inch (23–24-cm) fluted flan tin with it. Prick it all over the base with a fork and bake on the baking sheet near the top of the oven for 10 minutes, then remove the flan and increase the temperature of the oven to mark 5/375°F/190°C. Next carefully skin the fish, separate the flesh into large flakes, lay these over the base of the pastry case and squeeze a little lemon juice over the top. Now whisk the milk, eggs, mustard and freshly grated nutmeg together with some salt and pepper. Place the flan on the heated baking sheet in the centre of the oven, pour the liquid mixture carefully into it and sprinkle with cayenne pepper. Then bake for about 40 minutes until the filling is slightly puffed and golden. Served hot, warm or cold, it is delicious.

Salmon Fish Cakes (Serves 3)

I think tinned salmon makes very good fish cakes, as nice as if you'd used fresh.

A 7½-oz (210 g) tin salmon
½ lb (225 g) potatoes, peeled
2 tablespoons chopped parsley
2 gherkins, finely chopped
2 hardboiled eggs, chopped
2 teaspoons lemon juice
1 teaspoon anchovy essence
A good pinch cayenne pepper
Plain flour
Equal parts of oil and butter for frying
Salt and freshly milled black pepper

Begin by boiling the potatoes in salted water, then drain and mash them. Meanwhile drain the liquor from the salmon, discarding any skin or bones, and mash it to a paste with a fork. Then combine the potato with the fish, parsley, gherkins, hardboiled egg, lemon juice and anchovy essence. Mix everything thoroughly, taste and season with salt, freshly milled black pepper and cayenne. Next form the mixture into 6 fish cakes and dust each one with flour (all this can be done in advance). Then fry the fish cakes in the hot fat on both sides until golden. Drain and serve hot, garnished with sprigs of parsley and wedges of lemon.

Cold Marinated Mackerel   (Serves 2)

This makes a lovely summer dish to serve on a very hot day with, perhaps, some rice salad to accompany it.

2 good-sized fresh mackerel
1 lb (225 g) ripe tomatoes, skinned, de-seeded and chopped
1 small green pepper, de-seeded and finely chopped
1 small onion, peeled and finely chopped
½ small lemon, thinly sliced
¼ pint (150 ml) dry cider
3 tablespoons cider vinegar
4 tablespoons oil
½ teaspoon mixed herbs
2 level tablespoons chopped fresh parsley
Salt and freshly milled black pepper
2 pinches cayenne pepper

Have the fishmonger gut the mackerel for you, leaving the heads on. Wipe them clean with kitchen paper, then arrange the fish in an oval fireproof casserole just large enough to hold them side by side—alternatively, you could fit them into a frying pan. Now place the rest of the ingredients (except the parsley and seasonings) in a saucepan, cover and simmer for 20 minutes. Taste, season with salt, freshly milled black pepper and a couple of pinches of cayenne, then pour the mixture over the fish in the casserole. Now bring it up to the boil and simmer very gently for just 5 minutes. Turn the fish over very carefully, cover again and leave them to become quite cold in the juices in the casserole. Serve sprinkled with chopped fresh parsley.

Mackerel with Caper Sauce (Serves 2)

2 fresh mackerel, headed and gutted (get the fishmonger to do
   this for you)
5 tablespoons oil
1 large clove garlic, crushed
Juice of 1 large lemon
4 oz (110 g) capers, drained and coarsely crushed
Salt and freshly milled black pepper

A few hours before you need to cook the fish, put the oil in a
bowl with the crushed garlic and beat in the lemon juice,
followed by the capers and some salt and pepper. Then leave it
on one side for the flavours to develop. When you are ready to
cook the fish, remove the grill rack from the grill and line it
with foil. Pre-heat the grill and arrange the fish on the foil,
after gashing each side of the fish twice (in the thickest part of
their bodies). Sprinkle with salt and pepper, and pour the
caper sauce in and around the fish. Brush a little oil over each
one. Grill under a high heat so that the skins turn crisply
brown—they will need 3–4 minutes on each side. Then serve
with all the pan juices poured over. You'll need lots of crusty
bread to mop up the juices.

Tomato and Anchovy Quiche (Serves 4 as a main course)

This has a lovely Mediterranean flavour and tastes very good
eaten out of doors on a hot summer's day.

Shortcrust pastry (made with 6 oz/175 g plain flour and 3 oz/
   75 g fat, see page 212)
1 tablespoon olive oil
2 medium onions, peeled and finely chopped
1 clove garlic, crushed
1½ lb (700 g) tomatoes, skinned, de-seeded and chopped
1 teaspoon dried basil
A 2 oz (50 g) tin anchovy fillets
3 tablespoons tomato purée
2 tablespoons chopped parsley

2 eggs
1 oz (25 g) black olives, pitted and halved
2 tablespoons grated Parmesan cheese
Salt and freshly milled black pepper

Pre-heat the oven to mark 4/350°F/180°C

Begin by lining a 10-inch (25.5-cm) flan tin with the pastry, prick the base all over with a fork and pre-cook it on a baking sheet for 15 minutes. Then remove it from the oven and increase the heat to mark 5/375°F/190°C. Meanwhile heat the oil in a medium-sized saucepan and cook the finely chopped onion and crushed garlic over a gentle heat until softened but not coloured. Then stir in the chopped tomatoes and basil, and cook, uncovered, over a fairly high heat until the mixture is reduced to a thick consistency and most of the excess liquid has evaporated. Now drain the anchovies, retaining the oil from the can. Chop up 6 anchovies, then cut the rest in half lengthways and keep them on one side. Remove the pan from the heat and stir in the 6 chopped fillets, tomato purée and parsley; then beat the eggs together in a basin before stirring them into the tomato mixture. Taste and season with pepper and a little salt if it needs it. Now spread the mixture evenly in the pre-cooked flan case and decorate the top with a lattice-work of the remaining halved anchovy fillets. Then sprinkle over the pitted, halved black olives. Sprinkle the surface with the oil retained from the anchovy can and finally with the Parmesan cheese. Now bake for 40 minutes until the filling is puffed and is a light brown.

CHICKENS' LIB

Chicken is a problem. The cheapest form of chicken is the frozen variety, and most chickens sold in this country are frozen: being only 7–8 weeks old, they are also tasteless, and have probably been fed on fish protein (which has an alarming knack of impregnating a bird with a fishy flavour if not removed from the diet a month before the bird is killed). On the other hand, the best chicken to buy is the one that has been allowed to hang in the family butcher's and is drawn only at the point of purchase, but that is also the most expensive.

It's not quite as straightforward as that, though. Very many frozen chickens that come off the production line are eviscerated quickly, then plunged into a trough of iced water to be cooled rapidly. At the same time they absorb up to 10 per cent of their own weight in water and then are packed off to be frozen, water and all. You are in effect paying for 10 per cent water when you buy many frozen chickens.

Fortunately, there is an alternative to water-cooling, and that is air-cooling in which no water is absorbed to increase weight or extract flavour. That is why supermarket, fresh-chilled chickens don't have the bleached white look which so many mass-produced varieties have: they have that healthy pinkish tinge you find on fresh chickens hanging in butchers.

In short, if you can't get hold of a freshly drawn bird from a butcher, my advice is to plump for an air-chilled chicken— and in the interests of frugality, go back to the days when chicken was a *treat* by having fewer but better-flavoured ones. You can always make up the shortfall by having rabbit once in a while—now there's a neglected delicacy.

Chicken Pot Roast
(Serves 4–6)

Needless to say you'll need a freshly drawn chicken for this, and ask your supplier to be sure to give you the giblets.

A 3½-lb (1.6-kg) roasting chicken
1 largish onion, peeled and stuck with 3 cloves
4 leeks, trimmed and washed
4 carrots, scraped
4 sticks celery, halved
A few parsley stalks
1 bayleaf
1 clove garlic, crushed
Butter
Salt and freshly milled black pepper
2 tablespoons chopped parsley

Pre-heat the oven to mark 8/450°F/230°C

First rub the inside of the chicken with salt and pepper and a little butter. Then place the onion stuck with cloves inside the chicken and rub some butter and seasoning over the outside. Now put the chicken in a roasting tin and bake in the top half of the oven for about 30 minutes, by which time it should have developed a nice golden brown skin. Then remove it from the oven and transfer it, together with any juices, to a deep pot. Surround the chicken with the vegetables, herbs and garlic, and pour over sufficient water to not quite cover the bird, adding the giblets as well. Bring to boiling point and simmer very gently with the lid on for about 1 hour, or until the chicken is tender. Then remove the chicken and vegetables and cut the chicken into 4 portions; place the portions on a warmed serving dish surrounded by the vegetables, cover and keep warm. Now discard the giblets and boil the remaining stock briskly until it has reduced and the flavour has concentrated. Spoon some of the juices over the chicken and vegetables, sprinkle with chopped parsley and serve. Any stock left over can be used for soup.

Poulet à la Catalane

(Serves 6)

This is a good recipe if you're looking for an inexpensive dish for a special occasion, especially in the autumn when peppers and aubergines are at their cheapest.

1 fresh chicken (about 3½–4lb/1.6–1.8 kg), cut into 6 joints
2 oz (50 g) butter
Olive oil
8 fl oz (225 ml) dry cider
2 medium onions, peeled and chopped
1 clove garlic, crushed
3 small aubergines, cut into 1-inch (2.5-cm) cubes
2 medium green peppers, de-seeded and sliced
¼ lb (110 g) mushrooms, sliced
6 tomatoes, skinned, chopped and sliced
1 sprig fresh thyme
1 bayleaf
4 oz (110 g) Spanish stuffed olives, sliced
Salt and freshly milled black pepper

Pre-heat the oven to mark 5/375°F/190°C

In a large flameproof casserole heat the butter and 2 table-spoons of the oil together. Season the chicken joints and cook them to a nice golden brown, turning them over in the hot fat, then add the onions and the crushed garlic. Stir them around and let them cook for about 5–7 minutes. Now pour in the cider, let it bubble for a minute or two, add the thyme and bayleaf, then put the lid on and place the casserole in the oven to cook for about 45 minutes. Towards the end of that time, heat a little more of the oil in a frying pan and gently cook the chopped aubergines, peppers, tomatoes and mushrooms till soft, seasoning well with salt and freshly milled pepper. When the chicken is ready, take the casserole out of the oven, add all the vegetables plus the sliced olives and simmer the whole lot on top of the stove for about 5 minutes. Then spoon off any surplus fat, extract the thyme and bayleaf, and serve the chicken on a warmed serving dish, garnished if you like with little triangular croûtons of crisp-fried bread.

Devilled Chicken Drumsticks (Serves 3)

Supermarkets and good butchers do very reasonably priced packets of chicken drumsticks.

6 chicken drumsticks
2 tablespoons Worcestershire sauce
1 tablespoon tomato paste
1 tablespoon tomato ketchup
1 teaspoon made English mustard
1 teaspoon French mustard
1 teaspoon sugar
1 teaspoon soy sauce
1 teaspoon paprika
1 tablespoon oil
Salt and freshly milled black pepper

Start by arranging the chicken drumsticks in a single layer in the grill pan with the grid removed; then, using a skewer, stab the joints in several places. Now in a mixing bowl combine all the remaining ingredients together and stir thoroughly until smooth. Pour this mixture over the chicken and turn the pieces around in it. Then leave it, covered with foil, in a cool place for a minimum of 3 hours—or much longer if you like. To cook, pre-heat the grill, and then grill the chicken for about 15–20 minutes, or until the drumsticks are cooked. Keep turning them fairly frequently to prevent them burning, and serve very hot with any pan juices spooned over.

Pilau rice cooked with added chopped onion and green pepper (see page 157) is nice with this.

Chicken and Chick Peas   (Serves 4)

Chick peas give an unusual flavour to a chicken casserole as
well as making it more substantial, but they do need a long
soaking beforehand.

A 2½–3-lb (1.15–1.35-kg) roasting chicken, quartered
½ lb (225 g) chick peas, soaked overnight
1 oz (25 g) butter
2 tablespoons oil
1 large onion, peeled, halved and sliced
2 cloves garlic, crushed
A 14-oz (400-g) can Italian tomatoes
½ pint (275 ml) stock (made from the giblets)
1 bayleaf
1–2 tablespoons tomato purée
1 teaspoon dried basil
Salt and freshly milled black pepper

Pre-heat the oven to mark 3/325°F/170°C

To start with, the soaked and drained chick peas should be
placed in a saucepan with enough fresh water to cover them to a
depth of about 2 inches (5 cm) then brought to the boil. Simmer
(uncovered) for about 30 minutes, skimming after about 10
minutes—and don't bother to add any salt at this stage. While
that's happening, heat the butter and oil together in a flameproof
casserole, then dry the chicken quarters on kitchen paper and fry
in the hot fat over a medium heat until they're evenly browned.
Then, using a draining spoon, remove them to a plate and in the
fat remaining in the pan gently fry the sliced onion and crushed
garlic until softened. Now return the chicken joints to the pan
and pour over the contents of the can of tomatoes and the
chicken stock. Then drain the cooked chick peas, reserving their
cooking liquor. Now add them to the chicken mixture, with
¼ pint (150 ml) of the cooking liquor as well. Next add the bayleaf,
tomato purée and basil, and season with a little salt and pepper.
Bring up to simmering point, cover and transfer the casserole

to the oven. Bake for 30 minutes, then remove the lid and bake for a further 30 minutes. Taste the juices and add a bit more seasoning, if necessary, before serving. This dish is nice served with rice flavoured with onion.

Southern Fried Chicken (Serves 4)

I use the packets of chicken thighs or drumsticks for this, but you could use a 3-lb (1.35-kg) chicken cut in 8 pieces.

8 chicken joints
Groundnut oil for deep-frying
A little milk
4 oz (110 g) plain flour
½ teaspoon baking powder
Salt and freshly milled black pepper
Rock salt, crushed

Into a wide, deep pan pour enough oil to give a depth of 1 inch (2.5cm) and heat to 350°F/180°C, or until a small cube of bread turns crisp and golden in 1 minute. Meanwhile, dip the chicken pieces in milk. Mix the flour with the baking powder (I use a plastic bag), adding a good seasoning of salt and freshly milled black pepper. Jump the chicken joints up and down in the flour to coat them evenly. Now deep-fry them in the oil for 15 minutes, turning them over occasionally. When the chicken joints are cooked, drain them on crumpled greaseproof paper and serve immediately, sprinkled with a little crushed rock salt.

In America, Southern Fried Chicken has a traditional accompaniment of fried bananas and corn fritters. I think it's equally nice with some sauté potatoes and a crisp salad.

Spiced Chicken Pilau   (Serves 4)

Not all Indian dishes are as long and as complicated as one
would imagine: this one, for instance, can be made very easily
at home.

A 2½–3-lb (1.1–1.35-kg) roasting chicken, cut into 8 joints (plus
  chicken giblets)
2 tablespoons groundnut oil
2 medium onions, peeled and finely chopped
1 green pepper, de-seeded and finely chopped
2 cloves garlic, crushed
1 heaped teaspoon ground ginger
1 level teaspoon turmeric
1 level teaspoon Madras curry powder
1 inch (2.5 cm) cinnamon stick
¼ pint (150 ml) natural yoghurt
1 cup long-grain rice
2½ teacups chicken stock (made with the giblets)
2 bayleaves, crumbled
2 cloves
Salt and freshly milled black pepper

Wipe the chicken joints and season them with salt and pepper.
Heat the oil in a large saucepan or flameproof casserole and fry
the seasoned chicken joints until well browned. Then, using a
draining spoon, remove them to a plate and gently fry the
chopped onions, pepper and garlic in the fat remaining in the
pan. As soon as they're softened (about 6 minutes), stir in the
ginger, turmeric, curry powder and cinnamon, then return the
chicken joints to the pan and stir in the yoghurt. Cover the pan
and cook gently for about 15 minutes, giving it a shake from
time to time. Now uncover the pan and stir in the rice,
followed by the stock, bayleaf and cloves. Then bring to
simmering point, cover and cook gently for about 20 minutes. After that remove the pan from the heat and leave
(covered) until the rice has absorbed the excess liquid.
Now taste and season, if it needs it, and serve with some
mango chutney.

Mustard-coated Chicken (Serves 4)

It's best to prepare this 3–4 hours in advance so that the mustard flavours can penetrate the chicken.

8 small chicken joints (wings and thighs), or a whole chicken
  cut in 8
2 tablespoons made English mustard
1 tablespoon Dijon mustard
2 eggs
5 oz (150 g) dry white breadcrumbs
Plain flour
Salt and freshly milled black pepper
Cooking oil

Begin by removing the skins from the chicken joints, then in a small basin blend together smoothly both the mustards and the eggs. Now take 2 squares of greaseproof paper: on one place the breadcrumbs and on the other some flour. Season each chicken joint with freshly milled black pepper and salt, and dust with flour. Then dip each one into the mustard mixture (making sure it's evenly coated) and roll it in the breadcrumbs, patting the crumbs on firmly. Place all the joints on a large plate and chill for 3 or 4 hours. To cook the chicken you'll need either a very large frying pan or two smaller ones with about 1 inch (2.5 cm) of oil, heated to the stage where a small cube of bread froths on contact. Fry the chicken joints over a medium heat for about 20 minutes in all, turning them over occasionally—they should be crisp and golden. Drain on crumpled greaseproof paper and serve hot.

Spiced Chicken with Lentils (Serves 6)

For this recipe try to buy the whole brown or green lentils, and don't worry if you haven't got all the relevant spices, you can use curry powder instead—about 2 teaspoons of the hot Madras kind.

A $3\frac{1}{2}$-lb (1.6-kg) chicken, cut into 6 portions
2 tablespoons groundnut oil
2 medium onions, peeled and sliced
1 clove garlic, crushed
1 heaped teaspoon ground coriander
1 level teaspoon ground ginger
1 teaspoon ground cumin
1 level teaspoon turmeric
$\frac{1}{2}$-$\frac{3}{4}$ teaspoon chilli powder (depending on how hot you like it)
$\frac{1}{2}$ lb (225 g) whole lentils, soaked in cold water for half an hour
1 tablespoon tomato purée
$\frac{3}{4}$ pint (425 ml) chicken stock made with the giblets
Salt

Pre-heat the oven to mark 4/350°F/180°C

Start by heating the oil in a flameproof casserole and fry the chicken portions to a nice golden colour on all sides. Then set them on one side and add the onions and garlic to the pan. Soften them for about 5 minutes, then stir in the spices and cook for another 5 minutes. Now return the chicken pieces to the casserole and spoon the spicy onion and oil mixture over them. Next add the drained lentils, then mix the tomato purée with the hot chicken stock and pour that in. Now add a little salt and bring everything up to simmering point—and make sure all the lentils are pushed down so that they are almost covered by the liquid. Put a lid on and transfer the casserole to the oven, where it will take about 45 minutes to an hour to cook. Serve with rice and mango chutney.

Harvest Rabbit   (Serves 4)

If you live in the country, then you'll probably know that wild
rabbits are very often available at harvest time. However, if
you're not lucky enough to get a wild one, a commercially
reared one will do.

1 young rabbit, jointed
4 large carrots, scraped and cut into chunks
4 small onions, peeled and left whole
1 bayleaf
A sprig of thyme
A few parsley stalks
1 pint (570 ml) hot water (see below)
1 tablespoon chopped fresh parsley
Salt and freshly milled black pepper
1 tablespoon butter worked to a paste with 1 tablespoon plain
   flour

For the suet-crust pastry:
6 oz (175 g) self-raising flour
3 oz (75 g) shredded suet
1 teaspoon grated onion
1 tablespoon chopped fresh parsley
Salt and freshly milled black pepper

Pre-heat the oven to mark 4/350°F/180°C

Wash the rabbit joints first and place them in a 9½-inch (24-cm)
diameter casserole, season with pepper and salt, then scatter in
the herbs and tuck the carrots and onions in amongst them.
Now pour in the hot water, put a lid on and bake for 30
minutes; then remove the lid and bake for a further 30 minutes,
or until the rabbit is tender. Remove the rabbit from the oven
and increase the heat to mark 7/425°F/220°C. Add the flour
and butter paste, cut into peanut-sized pieces, plus the parsley,
and stir it in where possible. Now make up a suet-crust pastry
with the flour, suet, grated onion and parsley, seasoning with
pepper and salt. Add enough cold water to make an elastic
dough that leaves the bowl clean, then roll it out to fit inside the

79

casserole, covering the rabbit, etc. Now return the casserole to the oven for 25–35 minutes, or until the suet-crust is browned and puffy. Serve very hot with a green vegetable to go with it.

Note: You can improve this, if you have the time, by boiling the head and ribs to make 1 pint (570 ml) of stock to use instead of water, or use $\frac{1}{2}$ pint (275 ml) of dry cider and $\frac{1}{2}$ pint (275 ml) of water.

Rabbit in Cider   (Serves 4)

As in the previous recipe, if you can get hold of a wild rabbit for this, so much the better.

2 lb (900 g) rabbit joints (or a medium rabbit, jointed)
1 oz (25 g) butter
1 tablespoon oil
2 medium onions, peeled and chopped
1 clove garlic, crushed
$\frac{1}{2}$ lb (225 g) unsmoked streaky bacon, bought if possible in one
   piece and then cut in cubes
1 heaped tablespoon plain flour
$\frac{1}{2}$ pint (275 ml) dry cider
$\frac{1}{2}$ pint (275 ml) stock
A sprig of thyme (or $\frac{1}{2}$ teaspoon dried)
6 juniper berries, crushed
$\frac{1}{2}$ lb (225 g) dark-gilled mushrooms, sliced
Salt and freshly milled black pepper

Begin by heating the butter and oil in a flameproof casserole and frying the rabbit joints quickly to brown them all over. Now remove them to one side and fry the onions, garlic and bacon for about 10 minutes. Then sprinkle in the flour, stir and cook for a minute or two before gradually stirring in the cider and the stock. At this stage add the rabbit joints, together with the thyme and crushed juniper berries. Bring everything to simmering point, then add the sliced mushrooms and a seasoning of salt and freshly milled pepper. Cover and simmer the rabbit very gently for about an hour, or until it's tender.

Roasted Rabbit with Onions and Bacon

(Serves 4)

1 largish rabbit (ask the butcher to joint it for you)
2 large onions, peeled and chopped
$\frac{1}{2}$ lb (225 g) fat streaky bacon
$1\frac{1}{2}$ tablespoons seasoned plain flour
2 oz (50 g) dripping or butter
Salt and freshly milled black pepper

Pre-heat the oven to mark 4/350°F/180°C

Dust the rabbit joints with seasoned flour and wrap each joint in one or two rashers of streaky bacon. Now arrange them in a roasting tin and season with freshly milled black pepper and just a little salt (because there's some in the bacon). Tuck the pieces of onion in and around the rabbit (putting some pieces underneath the joints), then dot some little knobs of dripping or butter here and there. Place the roasting tin in the oven and cook for 1 hour, basting with the fat and juices at least 3 times. When it's ready, remove everything to a serving dish, spoon off the fat from the roasting tin and make a gravy to go with it.

FOREQUARTER FRONT

The figures are well known: it takes 10 lb (4.5 kg) of grain to get 1 lb (450 g) of beef. About 40–50 per cent of our beef is grain-fed, therefore each time there is a bad harvest world grain prices rocket (and so does beef). You don't have to be a monetary expert to see that it's a very wasteful way of intensively producing protein.

I don't think we should do without beef altogether, but as the world population increases—and grain shortages along with it—it would be unrealistic to think of the future of meat as anything but doubtful. TVP (see page 182) has now arrived and laboratory nutritionists are already investigating such phenomena as 'bacterial' proteins. As for us, well perhaps the affluent era of everyday steaks, chops and grills *is* on the way out, but by world standards we still have a lot of meat in this country. However, because it's going to cost us more and more, I feel that from now on we have to make the best possible use of it.

There's no such thing as cheap cuts any more, but forequarter meat (on me that's from the waist up) *is* less expensive and *does* get overlooked, since it needs more careful and longer cooking. Yet if you're prepared to take the trouble, forequarter meat very often has a far better flavour.

I promise that if you were to make a direct comparison you would find that shoulder of lamb has a sweeter flavour than leg: similarly, belly and shoulder of pork compared with leg. And silverside or topside are mere shadows of chuck when it comes to pot-roasting or braising. Flavour is not a feature of intensively reared meat at the best of times, so let us nurture what little we have (lamb being the one exception, of course—the only reliable species of 'free-range' meat left to us). So forward forequarters! as in the following recipes, which may take a little longer to cook but won't be difficult to prepare.

Braised Pork with Prunes (Serves 4)

$1\frac{1}{2}$ lb (700 g) lean belly of pork or spare ribs, cut into cubes
Lard
Salt and freshly milled black pepper
6 juniper berries, crushed
$\frac{1}{2}$ teaspoon chopped thyme
$\frac{1}{2}$ lb (225 g) onions, peeled and sliced
1 clove garlic, curshed
4 oz (110 g) prunes, halved and stoned
1 large cooking apple, peeled, cored and sliced
A little caster sugar
$1\frac{1}{2}$ lb (700 g) potatoes, peeled and thickly sliced
Butter
$\frac{1}{4}$ pint (150 ml) dry cider

Pre-heat the oven to mark 3/325°F/170°C

Fry the pork in a little lard to brown it nicely, then arrange it in the bottom of a shallow (and fairly wide) fireproof casserole or pie dish. Season with pepper and salt and sprinkle over the crushed juniper berries and the chopped thyme. Now fry the onion and garlic a little bit, and put it round the pork with a few pieces of prune tucked here and there. Next arrange the apple slices all over and give them a very slight dusting of caster sugar. Finally, arrange the thick potato slices on top, making them overlap one another. Season with some more pepper and salt, dot with a few flecks of butter and pour in the cider. Cover and bake for $1\frac{1}{2}$ hours. When the cooking time's up, raise the heat to mark 8/450°F/230°C, remove the lid and cook for a further 20 minutes or so—or until the potatoes have turned a lovely golden brown (or brown them under a hot grill).

Roast Lamb with Coriander (Serves 3)

In the winter, when only imported lamb is reasonably priced, this is a good way to jazz up half a shoulder.

½ shoulder of lamb
1 clove garlic, cut into slivers
1 tablespoon coriander seeds
Dripping
Stock or dry cider

Pre-heat the oven to mark 5/375°F/190°C

Place the meat in a roasting tin and, using a small sharp knife, make about 6–8 evenly placed incisions in it. Into these slits push slivers of garlic and the coriander seeds (crushed a bit first, using either a pestle and mortar or the back of a tablespoon). Add a knob of dripping to the roasting tin and roast for 30 minutes to the pound (450 g), basting with the juices from time to time. When the lamb is cooked, carve it into thick slices and keep warm. Then strain off the fat from the roasting tin and add a little stock or dry cider to the juices to make a gravy. Redcurrant jelly is a nice accompaniment.

Beef in Cider

This is an inexpensive dish, although special enough for a dinner party—quite simply a classic boeuf bourguignonne only made with cider and every bit as good.

2 lb (900 g) chuck steak, cut into largish chunks
Beef dripping
1 medium onion, peeled and sliced
1 rounded tablespoon plain flour
$\frac{3}{4}$ pint (420 ml) dry cider
2 cloves garlic, chopped
2 sprigs fresh thyme (or $\frac{1}{2}$ teaspoon dried)
1 bayleaf
Salt and freshly milled black pepper
$\frac{3}{4}$ lb (350 g) small onions, peeled and left whole
$\frac{1}{2}$ lb (225 g) streaky bacon in one piece (smoked or green)
$\frac{1}{4}$ lb (110 g) dark flat mushrooms, sliced

Pre-heat the oven to mark 2/300°F/150°C

Start off by melting some beef dripping in a very large solid frying pan and frying the sliced onion for 5 minutes. Then turn the heat right up, add the cubes of meat and brown them quickly on all sides, tossing them around frequently. Next sprinkle in the flour, stir it around to soak up all the juices, then gradually pour in the cider—stirring all the time—and add the chopped garlic and herbs. Season with salt and pepper, then pour the whole lot into a casserole, put a lid on and cook in the oven for 2 hours. Now, using a bit more beef dripping, fry the small onions and bacon to colour them lightly, and add them to the casserole together with the sliced mushrooms. Then put the lid back on and cook for a further hour. This is nice served with buttered noodles or onion-flavoured rice (see pages 160 or 157).

Pork and Kidney Hotpot

(Serves 3–4)

I love to use juniper berries with pork dishes, but if you haven't got—or can't get—any, just leave them out.

1 lb (450 g) lean belly of pork, cut into cubes
1 pork kidney, trimmed and sliced
1 medium cooking apple, peeled and thinly sliced
1 largish onion, peeled and chopped
2 tablespoons well-seasoned plain flour
½ teaspoon dried sage
1 clove garlic, crushed
2 lb (900 g) potatoes, peeled and thickly sliced
½ pint (275 ml) stock or dry cider
Lard
A little melted butter
Salt and freshly milled black pepper

Pre-heat the oven to mark 5/375°F/190°C

Melt some lard in a largish frying pan, then dust the pieces of pork in seasoned flour and fry them to a nice golden brown all round. Now, using a draining spoon, transfer them to a pie dish (I use an old pie dish of about 2½ pints/1.5 litres capacity). Next fry the slices of kidney (which should also have been dipped in seasoned flour) and tuck those in amongst the pork; then sprinkle the sage over the pork, followed by some salt and pepper. Now soften the onion and garlic in the frying pan for about 10 minutes, then sprinkle them over the meat, followed by the slices of apple. Next pour in the stock or cider and finally top everything with the slices of potato overlapping each other. Season the potatoes, brush them with a little melted butter and bake the hotpot in the oven for approximately 1 hour, or until the potatoes are a golden brown and the pork is tender.

Baked Stuffed Breast of Lamb

(Serves 2)

For this ask your butcher for a nice large breast of lamb and have him remove the bones for you.

1 large breast of lamb, boned

For the stuffing:
2 oz (50 g) fresh breadcrumbs
1 medium onion, peeled and very finely chopped
1 tablespoon chopped fresh parsley
1 tablespoon chopped fresh mint
1 teaspoon finely crushed rosemary
$\frac{1}{4}$ whole nutmeg, grated
Grated rind of $\frac{1}{2}$ lemon
Salt and freshly milled black pepper

Pre-heat the oven to mark 4/350°F/180°C

In a mixing bowl, mix the breadcrumbs and onion, parsley, mint and rosemary, then add the nutmeg and lemon rind. Mix thoroughly and add a good seasoning of pepper and salt. Now stir in the beaten egg to bind the stuffing together, then spread the stuffing evenly over the breast of lamb and roll the lamb up gently and not too tightly. Tuck the flap end over and tie the meat in 3 places with string—again not too tightly. Press back any bits of stuffing that fall out, wrap the meat in foil, place it on a roasting tin and bake for 1$\frac{1}{2}$ hours. Then unwrap the foil, baste with the juices and brown for a further $\frac{1}{2}$ hour, basting again once or twice. Serve the meat cut in thick slices with thin gravy made with the juices, and some red-currant jelly.

Pork Rissoles with Spiced Apple Sauce

(Serves 4)

These are lovely served with creamy mashed potatoes and cooked dried peas.

1 lb (450 g) shoulder of pork, cut into chunks
1 onion, peeled and quartered
4 oz (110 g) breadcrumbs (white or brown)
1 cooking apple, peeled, cored and quartered
½ teaspoon dried sage
¼ teaspoon ground mace
1 teaspoon salt
Freshly milled black pepper
A little butter

For the sauce
½ small onion, peeled and chopped
1 oz (25 g) butter
½ lb (225 g) cooking apples, peeled and chopped
1 tablespoon water
Freshly grated nutmeg
A couple of pinches ground cloves
Sugar to taste

Pre-heat the oven to mark 5/375°F/190°C

Pass the pork, onion, bread and apple through a mincer and mix them thoroughly with the remaining rissole ingredients. Form the mixture into balls and arrange in the base of a small buttered roasting tin. Cover with some buttered foil and bake in the top half of the oven for 45 minutes. Then remove the foil, raise the oven temperature to mark 6/400°F/200°C and continue to bake for a further 30 minutes, basting now and then, until the rissoles are nicely browned on top. Meanwhile, to make the sauce, soften the onion in the butter for 10 minutes, then stir in the sliced apple and the water. Put a lid on and simmer till soft, then add a little freshly grated nutmeg, a couple of pinches of ground cloves and enough sugar to taste. Beat the sauce till fluffy, and serve hot with the rissoles.

Shoulder of Lamb Stuffed with Rice and Olives

(Serves 4)

3–5 lb (1.35–2.25 kg) shoulder of lamb (ask the butcher to bone it for you and give you the trimmings)
2 oz (50 g) chopped onion
3 oz (75 g) rice, cooked (that's 3 oz (75 g) weight before cooking)
3–4oz (75–110g) minced lamb, from the trimmings
12 Spanish stuffed olives (6 of them quartered or sliced for the stuffing)
1 egg, beaten
1 clove garlic, crushed
2 tablespoons chopped parsley
$\frac{1}{4}$ teaspoon finely crushed rosemary
Salt and freshly milled pepper

For the gravy:
$\frac{3}{4}$ oz (20 g) plain flour
$\frac{1}{2}$ pint (275 ml) stock

Pre-heat the oven to mark 6/400°F/200°C

Begin by seasoning the inside surfaces of the meat with the crushed rosemary, salt and pepper. Then mix the minced lamb with the crushed garlic, cooked rice, chopped onion, chopped olives, parsley and a little of the beaten egg. Spread the stuffing over the meat, then roll the meat up as neatly as possible into a cylindrical shape. Now tie loops of string round it at 2-inch (5-cm) intervals, and season the surface with salt and pepper. Next place the meat in a roasting tin and roast the joint for 25 minutes to the pound. When it's cooked, remove the string and place it on a warmed serving dish to keep it warm whilst you make up the gravy. Using the juices in the pan, stir in the flour, then add the stock bit by bit, followed by the whole olives. Serve the meat with the gravy separate—and some new carrots and new potatoes would be a nice accompaniment.

Pot Roast of Pork with Cabbage and Juniper

(Serves 6–8)

An obliging butcher will bone and roll a shoulder joint for you for this.

3 lb (1.35 kg) shoulder of pork, boned and rolled
1¼ lb (575 g) white cabbage
3 tablespoons pork dripping (or lard)
2 medium onions, peeled and sliced
1 clove garlic, sliced
2 carrots, scraped and sliced
¼ teaspoon dried thyme (or a sprig of fresh)
12 juniper berries, crushed
A little chopped parsley
Salt and freshly milled black pepper

Pre-heat the oven to mark 3/325°F/160°C

Wipe the joint as dry as possible, then melt the dripping in an extra large flameproof casserole and, with the heat fairly high, brown the pork steadily all over. Then remove it to a plate while you fry the sliced onions, garlic and carrots for about 10 minutes or so. Now replace the joint in the casserole and bring it up to sizzling point. Sprinkle it with salt, pepper, the dried thyme and the juniper berries, then put a lid on and transfer it to the oven to bake for 1 hour, giving it a basting with the juices, about halfway through the cooking time. Meanwhile slice the cabbage. Bring a large saucepan of salted water to the boil, add the sliced cabbage, bring back to the boil to cook for 3 minutes, then rinse in cold water and drain in a colander, pressing out any excess liquid. When the hour is up, remove the casserole from the oven, add the drained cabbage and stir it into the juices in the casserole. Now re-heat until bubbling, cover again and replace in the oven for a further hour (once more basting the joint midway). When the time's up, remove the joint and slice into serving pieces, and taste and season the cabbage mixture. Arrange the sliced pork over the cabbage, sprinkle with chopped parsley and serve with some crunchy roast potatoes.

Pork with Summer Vegetables (Serves 2)

Because lamb is so popular during the summer months, pork is very often down in price. (Let's hope!)

2 spare rib chops
4 small or 2 large new carrots, scraped and sliced
6 shallots or small onions, peeled and left whole
$\frac{3}{4}$ lb (350 g) fresh peas (weighed in the pods)
1 dessertspoon lard
$\frac{1}{2}$ teaspoon chopped rosemary (fresh if possible)
$\frac{1}{4}$ pint (150 ml) boiling water
Salt and freshly milled black pepper

Pre-heat the oven to mark 3/325°F/170°C

First heat the lard in a frying pan and brown the chops, colouring them a nice golden brown on both sides. Then transfer them to a large ovenproof dish (I use a 3-pint/1.75-litre oval pie dish) and sprinkle them with the rosemary. Now add the whole shallots and the sliced carrots to the pan, and cook to colour them a little too. Then, using a draining spoon, arrange them round the pork, season and pour in $\frac{1}{4}$ pint (150 ml) of boiling water. Cover the dish with a double sheet of foil (or a lid) and transfer to the oven for an hour. Meanwhile shell the peas. When the hour is up, stir the peas down into the juices, taste and add a little more seasoning, if necessary; then re-cover with the foil and cook for an extra 20–30 minutes, depending on the age of the peas. Serve with new potatoes tossed in butter and snipped chives.

Note: If you can't get any small onions, use a couple of ordinary sized, sliced.

Mutton Pot Pie

(Serves 4)

The bones in the meat give this a delicious sauce, whilst the suet crust on top makes it very filling and substantial—in fact, don't plan to do anything much for a while after eating it.

8 large pieces middle neck of lamb
2 medium onions, peeled and chopped
3 medium carrots, scraped and sliced
1 lb (450 g) potatoes, peeled and sliced
2 tablespoons pearl barley
1 teaspoon dried thyme
1 clove garlic, crushed
2 tablespoons seasoned plain flour
Salt and freshly milled black pepper

For the suet-crust pastry:
8 oz (225 g) self-raising flour
4 oz (110 g) shredded suet
Salt and freshly milled black pepper

Pre-heat the oven to mark 2/300°F/150°C

Trim any excess fat from the lamb, then dust the pieces with seasoned flour and arrange a layer of meat in the bottom of a heavy flameproof casserole, about 4 pints (2.25 litres) capacity, followed by a sprinkling of the crushed garlic and thyme, then a layer of vegetables and a tablespoon of pearl barley. Season well. Repeat the layers and finally add enough boiling water to almost cover everything. Then put on the lid and cook in the oven for about 2 hours. Just before the end of the cooking time, make the pastry by mixing the flour and suet with some pepper, salt and just enough cold water to make a smooth, elastic dough. Now remove the casserole and turn the heat right up to mark 7/425°F/220°C. Roll the pastry out to a round big enough to just fit inside the rim of the casserole. Put it on and make a small hole in the centre. Return the casserole to the oven (without a lid this time) and let the pastry cook for 30 minutes. Serve immediately.

Brown Beef Stew with Dumplings   (Serves 4)

1 lb (450 g) of chuck steak will serve 4 easily in this recipe, which includes plenty of vegetables *and* some fluffy dumplings.

1 lb (450 g) chuck steak, cubed
2 oz (50 g) beef dripping
4 smallish onions, peeled and left whole
1 medium turnip, peeled and cut into chunks
½ swede, peeled and cut into chunks
6 small carrots, scraped and left whole
A knob of butter
1½ tablespoons plain flour
1½ pint (570 ml) boiling water
1 bayleaf
½ teaspoon dried mixed herbs
1½ teaspoons Worcestershire sauce
Salt and freshly milled black pepper

For the dumplings:
4 oz (110 g) self-raising flour
2 oz (50 g) shredded suet
1 tablespoon fresh chopped parsley
Salt and freshly milled black pepper

Pre-heat the oven to mark 2/300°F/150°C

For this you'll need a flameproof 4½–5 pint (2.5–2.95 litre) casserole and a large frying pan. First of all you heat the dripping till smoking hot and brown the pieces of meat in it quickly, tossing them around—they should be a deep brown, nutty colour. Now take a draining spoon and transfer them to the casserole. Then, lowering the heat a little, start to fry the prepared vegetables. These, too, should be browned and caramelised a bit at the edges (this is very important for the flavour of the stew). As they brown, transfer them to the casserole to join the meat. Now to the juices left in the frying pan add a knob of butter, allow it to melt, then stir in the flour and, with the heat reasonably high, keep stirring and let the flour get brown before gradually adding the hot water, still stirring, as you would for white sauce. When you've added all the water, pour this gravy into the casserole over the meat and vegetables, add some salt and pepper, the bayleaf, herbs and Worcestershire sauce, put a tight lid on and transfer it to the oven to cook for 3 hours.

Just before the end of the cooking time, sift the flour into a basin, mix in the suet, parsley, pepper and salt, and enough cold water to make a smooth elastic dough that leaves the bowl clean. Then divide the dough and roll it into 10 or 12 small balls. Now transfer the casserole to the top of the stove, give it a gentle heat to keep it just simmering, then pop the dumplings in all over the top (don't push them into the liquid, just sit them on top). Put the lid back on, and let the stew simmer for 25 minutes. Then serve immediately—one snag with dumplings is that they don't like hanging around.

Porc au Chou
(Serves 3–4)

Try to get lean belly of pork cut from the thick end; alternatively, you could use cubed spare rib chops.

1¼ lb (570 g) belly of pork, cubed
4 oz/(110 g) streaky bacon, rinded and cut into small cubes
1 large onion, peeled and chopped
1 clove garlic, crushed
2 tablespoons oil
10 juniper berries, crushed
½ pint (275 ml) dry cider
1 lb (450 g) white cabbage, shredded
Chopped fresh parsley
Salt and freshly milled black pepper.

Pre-heat the oven to mark 3/325°F/170°C

Heat the oil in a flameproof casserole and soften the onion and garlic in it for about 5 minutes. Then add the cubes of bacon and pork and, with the heat fairly high, brown them to a golden colour, tossing them frequently around. Now lower the heat, add the shredded cabbage and stir to get it all nicely coated with oil; then add the crushed juniper berries followed by the cider. Season with salt and pepper, then put a tight-fitting lid on and cook in the oven for about 1–1¼ hours.

Although this tastes very good, its appearance is deceptive and needs a sprinkling of chopped parsley to 'jazz' it up a bit.

Steak and Onions in Guinness (Serves 2)

If you long for a thick, juicy, grilled steak and can't afford it, try this recipe with braising steak—it's every bit as good.

¾–1 lb (350–450g) lean braising steak (in 2 pieces)
2 large onions, peeled and cut into rings
¼ pint (150 ml) Guinness
Beef dripping
Salt and freshly milled black pepper

Pre-heat the oven to mark 2/300°F/150°C

In a frying pan melt a little dripping and fry the onion rings over a medium heat until they're nicely tinged with brown and starting to caramelise all round the edges. Now remove them to a plate, add a little more dripping to the pan if you need to and brown the meat over a fairly high heat. This browning (on both sides) will help the flavour. Next take a shallow gratin dish or casserole, arrange a layer of onion in it, place the steak on top and season well. Add another layer of onion, pour in the Guinness, cover closely with either a lid or a double sheet of foil and cook near the top of the oven for 2½–3 hours, or until the steak is tender. This goes very well with some creamed potatoes—and with the oven on for that length of time, you might contemplate cooking another casserole at the same time.

Devilled Pork Slices (Serves 3)

For this ask the butcher for 6 lean slices of pork cut from the thick end of the belly.

6 lean slices belly of pork (about 1¼ lb/570 g)
Salt and freshly milled black pepper

For the sauce:
1 tablespoon tomato purée
1 tablespoon water
1 tablespoon Worcestershire sauce
1 tablespoon wine vinegar
1 teaspoon clear honey
1 teaspoon made English mustard
1 clove garlic, crushed
1 level dessertspoon ground ginger
Salt and freshly milled black pepper

Pre-heat the oven to mark 6/400°F/200°C

Trim the rind and any excess fat from the pork, arrange the slices in a single layer in a roasting tin and season them a little. Then thoroughly combine all the sauce ingredients together in a basin and pour this mixture over the pork. Cover the tin with foil and bake in the oven for about 40 minutes. After that, remove the foil and bake for a further 20 minutes or so. Now arrange the pork slices on a warmed serving dish. Keep them warm whilst you spoon off any fat from the roasting tin, then add about 4 tablespoons of hot water (potato water would be ideal) and stir over a medium heat, scraping the sides and base of the tin. When it reaches simmering point, pour the gravy over the pork and serve with creamy mashed potato.

Ground Beef Curry   (Serves 3)

This is a good way to 'uplift' 1lb (450g) of mince, but it *has* to be good-quality mince from a reliable supplier.

1 lb (450g) good-quality minced beef
$\frac{3}{4}$ lb (350g) onions, peeled and sliced
1 small apple, finely chopped
2 tablespoons groundnut oil
2 cloves garlic, crushed
1 dessertspoon Madras curry powder (or more or less, depending on how hot you like it)
$\frac{1}{2}$ teaspoon ground ginger
$\frac{1}{2}$ teaspoon turmeric
$\frac{1}{4}$ pint (150ml) natural yoghurt
$\frac{1}{4}$ pint (150ml) hot water mixed with 1 heaped teaspoon tomato purée
Salt and freshly milled black pepper

Pre-heat the oven to mark 2/300°F/150°C

First of all, in a flameproof casserole, heat the oil and soften the sliced onions in it for about 10 minutes. Then turn up the heat, stir in the minced beef and move it around until it's all nicely browned and separate—a wooden fork is good for this. Now turn the heat down, and stir in the apple and spices, garlic and some salt and pepper, followed by the yoghurt and the tomato-and-water mixture. Stir thoroughly, put a lid on and cook in the oven for 2 hours. Serve with rice and mango chutney.

Note: This *could* be cooked on top of the stove if watched carefully.

Fidget Pie

There are many versions of this famous English dish. I don't claim this recipe to be the authentic one, but it's very good.

1½ lb (700 g) boned gammon forehock
¾ lb (350 g) onions, peeled, halved and very thinly sliced
¾ lb (350 g) cooking apples, peeled, cored and sliced
1 lb (450 g) potatoes, peeled and very thinly sliced
Freshly milled black pepper (but no salt)
½ pint (275 ml) dry cider or hot water

For the pastry:
8 oz (225 g) plain flour
4 oz (110 g) lard
A pinch of salt
Water to mix
Milk to glaze

Pre-heat the oven to mark 5/375°F/190°C

First remove the rind and excess fat from the gammon, and cut the meat into quite small pieces. Then gather together all the rest of the ingredients for the pie, take a large 3½-pint (2-litre) pie dish and layer the ingredients in this order: first the gammon, then the onions and apples and finally the pota-toes—about 3 layers of each, finishing off with a layer of potatoes. As you go, sprinkle a little freshly milled pepper in between the layers. Now pour in the cider. Next prepare the pastry as described on page 212, and roll it out. Line the rim of the pie dish with pastry strips and dampen them before covering with a pastry lid. Now pinch the edges to seal, and decorate the top of the pie (any pastry left over can be re-rolled and cut into pastry 'leaves'). Lastly, brush the pastry with milk, make a steam hole in the centre of the pie and sit the pie dish on a baking sheet. After 30 minutes reduce the heat to mark 3/325°F/170°C and cook for a further hour.

Bacon with Dumplings and Parsley Sauce

(Serves 4)

This is both filling and comforting on a really cold day.

A piece of bacon collar weighing about 1½ lb (700 g)
1 bayleaf
A few parsley stalks
4 smallish onions, peeled and left whole
2 large carrots, scraped and cut in half

For the dumplings:
3 oz (75 g) self-raising flour
1½ (40 g) oz shredded suet
Salt and freshly milled black pepper

For the sauce:
1 oz (25 g) butter
1 oz (25 g) plain flour
¼ pint (150 ml) milk
½ pint (275 ml) stock (use the bacon water)
2 heaped tablespoons chopped fresh parsley

Place the bacon in a good *large* casserole (it must be large enough to take all the other things). Then cover with cold water, bring to the boil and throw out the water. This will take care of any saltiness. Now pour on some fresh boiling water to just cover the bacon, add the bayleaf and a few parsley stalks, put a lid on and simmer gently for 30 minutes. Then add the peeled whole onions and halved carrots, replace the lid and continue simmering for a further 20 minutes. Meanwhile make the dumplings by mixing the flour, suet and some seasoning with enough cold water to make a smooth elastic dough, and roll it into 8 small dumplings. When the 20 minutes' cooking time is up, ladle out ½ pint (275 ml) of the bacon stock into a measuring jug. Then, keeping the rest simmering, pop the dumplings in around the bacon—don't push them down, let them float—cover and cook for a further 25 minutes. Meanwhile make a parsley sauce with the butter, flour, milk, reserved bacon stock (plus a little extra if you need it) and the chopped parsley. Serve the bacon cut in slices with the onion, dumplings and carrots, and the sauce in a jug.

Navarin of Lamb (Serves 4)

This is an excellent way of serving middle neck of lamb. I like it best made in the summer with new potatoes, but it can be made in the winter using chunks of old potatoes instead.

2 lb (900 g) middle neck of lamb, cut into pieces
Dripping
2 tablespoons plain flour
1¼ pints (725 ml) hot water
1 level tablespoon tomato purée
1 clove garlic, crushed
½ teaspoon dried thyme (or a sprig of fresh thyme)
8 small onions, peeled and left whole
6 baby turnips, peeled and quartered
6 small carrots, scraped and cut into 1-inch (2–5 cm) lengths
12 very small new potatoes, scraped
1 level teaspoon brown sugar
Salt and freshly milled black pepper

Begin by heating some dripping in a large flameproof casserole. Trim any excess fat from the meat, then season the pieces with salt and pepper, and fry them in the hot fat until brown on all sides. Now sprinkle in the flour and, keeping the heat fairly low, stir it around to soak up the juices. Next add the hot water, tomato purée, crushed garlic and thyme. Then bring everything gently up to simmering point, giving it a stir now and then. Put the lid on and cook very gently for 45 minutes. While that's happening, using a little more dripping fry the prepared onions, turnips and carrots. When the 45 minutes is up, add these vegetables to the casserole along with the scraped potatoes and bring to simmering point again. Add the sugar, cover and continue to simmer gently for a further 45 minutes.

Pork Chops Boulangère

(Serves 4)

For this you can also use spare rib chops or belly of pork strips.

4 pork chops (see above)
4 large potatoes, peeled and thinly sliced
1 large onion, peeled and finely chopped
1 tablespoon seasoned plain flour
$\frac{3}{4}$ teaspoon dried sage
$\frac{1}{4}$ pint (150 ml) milk
$\frac{1}{2}$ pint (275 ml) stock (or water)
1 tablespoon oil
$\frac{1}{2}$ oz (10 g) butter, plus a little extra
Salt and freshly milled black pepper

Pre-heat the oven to mark 4/350°F/180°C

Dust the chops in seasoned flour, heat the $\frac{1}{2}$ oz (10 g) of butter and the oil in a large frying pan and fry the chops on both sides until nicely browned. Then remove the pan from the heat. Now butter a small roasting tin and put a layer of half the potatoes and onion over the base, seasoning them with salt and pepper. Lay the browned chops on top and sprinkle them with sage, salt and pepper. Cover them with the rest of the onions and then with a final layer of sliced potatoes. Next pour over the mixed stock and milk, add a few flecks of extra butter, cover with greased foil and bake in the oven for about an hour. Then take off the foil, raise the heat to mark 5/375°F/190°C for a further $\frac{1}{2}-\frac{3}{4}$ hour, or until the potatoes are browned on top. This is delicious served with spiced red cabbage.

Boiled Bacon and Pease Pudding

(Serves 6)

Try to get green split peas for this, but yellow will do if you can't buy the green.

A 2¾-lb (1.2-kg) piece boned rolled bacon forehock
1 onion, peeled, halved and each half stuck with 2 cloves
1 large carrot, scraped and cut in chunks
1 bayleaf
A few parsley stalks
1 lb (450 g) green split peas
2 oz (50 g) butter
¼–½ teaspoon caster sugar
Salt and freshly milled black pepper

Start off by placing the bacon in a large deep pot and covering it with cold water; then bring it to the boil and as soon as the water reaches boiling point, throw it out and start again with a new lot of cold water. Then add the onion, carrot, bayleaf and parsley stalks. Now wash the peas in a sieve and put them in a large section of linen cloth or double gauze (about 17 inches/43 cm square). Tie it very tightly, but leave the peas plenty of room to expand during the cooking, then pop the bundle of peas into the pot to cook alongside the bacon. Now put a lid on, bring to simmering point, then turn the heat down and simmer gently for about 1¼ hours. After that, have ready a bowl (warmed) containing the butter. Switch off the heat under the pot, remove the bundle of peas, untie it and scrape the peas into the warmed bowl. Now mash them to a purée. Taste and add the sugar, salt and freshly milled pepper, and if you think the mixture is still on the dry side, add a spoonful of the cooking liquor to moisten it while you skin and carve the bacon. Serve the bacon with the pease pudding on the table for everyone to help themselves—and some parsley sauce would make it extra specially good.

Traditional Cornish Pasties

The quantities given here will make 4 large pasties for 4 people; alternatively, smaller ones could be made for taking on a journey or picnic.

1 lb (450 g) chuck steak
1 medium potato, peeled and cut into very thin slices
1 large onion, peeled and chopped very small
1 medium turnip, peeled and cut into very thin slices
$\frac{1}{2}$ teaspoon mixed herbs
Salt and freshly milled black pepper
1 lb (450 g) shortcrust pastry (made with 10 oz/275 g plain
   flour, 5 oz/150 g lard, a pinch each salt and pepper, cold
   water to mix)
1 egg, beaten

Pre-heat the oven to mark 7/425°F/220°C

Cut the steak up into very small thin pieces and mix it with the potato, onion, turnip and herbs, seasoning well with salt and freshly milled black pepper. Then make the pastry (see page 212), divide it into 4 and roll each piece out on a lightly floured surface to a round approximately 8 inches (20 cm) in diameter. Place a quarter of the meat mixture in the centre of each round of pastry, then dampen the edges with beaten egg, pull them up to meet in the centre and seal them very thoroughly. Knock up the edges and flute them, then brush the pasties all over with beaten egg, make two small steam holes in each one and place all 4 of them on a lightly greased baking sheet and bake in the oven for 15 minutes. Then reduce the heat to mark 4/350°F/180°C and continue cooking them for another 60 minutes.

Steak and Kidney Hotpot   (Serves 6)

If you love the delicious combination of steak and kidney but
aren't too keen on suet pastry, then this recipe is for you,
because instead of pastry it has a crust of thickly sliced
potatoes on top.

1½ lb (700 g) chuck steak, trimmed and cut into bite-sized
    cubes
½ lb (225 g) ox kidney, trimmed and cut fairly small
2 lb (900 g) potatoes, peeled and cut into thick slices
2 medium onions, peeled and roughly chopped
1 rounded tablespoon plain flour
½ pint (275 ml) beef stock
¾ teaspoon Worcestershire sauce
Beef dripping
Melted butter
Salt and freshly milled black pepper

Pre-heat the oven to mark 2/300°F/150°C

First melt some beef dripping in a large, wide-based saucepan
and fry the onion in it to soften for about 5 minutes or so; then
turn the heat right up, add the cubes of beef and kidney and
cook them to a nutty brown colour—keep stirring and turning
the meat as it browns. Now lower the heat a bit, sprinkle in the
flour and stir it around to soak up the meat juices. Season well,
add the Worcestershire sauce, then gradually stir in the stock
and bring to simmering point. Next pour the meat mixture
into a casserole or pie dish and arrange the thickly sliced
potatoes in layers all over the meat. Season the potatoes, brush
them with melted butter, then cover the casserole with a lid or
foil and bake in the oven for 2½–3 hours. Before serving remove
the lid and brown the potatoes under a very hot grill to get
them really crisp.

Beef and Tomato Stew

(Serves 4–6)

This is a good recipe for using up over-ripe tomatoes that are too soft for a salad.

2 lb (900 g) chuck steak
3 tablespoons oil
2 onions, peeled and chopped
1 fat clove garlic, crushed
1 lb (450 g) tomatoes, skinned and thickly sliced
1 heaped teaspoon dried basil
$\frac{1}{2}$ teaspoon brown sugar
Salt and freshly milled black pepper

Pre-heat the oven to mark 2/300°F/150°C

First trim the meat, then cut it into 1–1$\frac{1}{2}$-inch (2.5–4 cm) cubes. Then heat the oil in a flameproof casserole and fry the meat over a fairly high heat until the cubes are nicely browned. Now add the chopped onions and garlic to the pan, turn the heat down a bit and continue to cook for a further 10 minutes, or until the onions are softened. Next add the tomatoes to the casserole with the basil and some salt and freshly milled black pepper. Stir well, cover the casserole and transfer to the oven to cook slowly for about 2–2$\frac{1}{2}$ hours, or until the meat is tender. Then taste and sprinkle in the sugar, and additional salt and freshly milled black pepper if it needs it. This is delicious served with buttered noodles.

Baked Stuffed Cabbage Leaves (Serves 4–5)

This is an anglicised version of the Greek dolmades—stuffed vine leaves.

A 2–3lb (900-g–1.35-kg) head of green cabbage
1 tablespoon oil
1 tablespoon butter
1 onion, peeled and finely chopped
1 clove garlic, crushed
1 lb (450 g) lean minced chuck steak
2 oz (50 g) rice, cooked (that's 2 oz (50 g) raw weight)
1 tablespoon tomato purée
1 tablespoon chopped parsley
$\frac{1}{2}$ teaspoon dried marjoram
$\frac{1}{2}$ teaspoon ground cinnamon
Salt and freshly milled black pepper
A 14 oz (400 g) can Italian tomatoes

Pre-heat the oven to mark 3/325°F/170°C

First bring a large saucepan of salted water to the boil and place the cabbage in the water, stalk end up. Next bring the water back to the boil and simmer for about 8 minutes; then remove the cabbage and leave it to cool. Working with the cabbage still stalk end up, take a sharp knife and cut the large outer leaves from the main stalk and peel them off one by one. Drain the leaves on kitchen paper—you'll need about 15 leaves altogether. The centre can be used for something else. Now heat the oil and butter together and fry the chopped onion with the garlic gently until the onion is soft and golden. Then add the minced beef and brown it, turning the heat up a bit. Then mix in the rice, parsley, cinnamon, marjoram and tomato purée, seasoning well. Remove the pan and let the mixture cool. Now make a V-shaped cut to remove the thickest part of the stalk from the base of each leaf, place about a tablespoon of stuffing in the centre of each leaf, fold in the sides and roll the leaf up tightly. Then pack the rolled leaves closely together in a casserole and pour the can of tomatoes over; cover and cook in the oven for 1$\frac{1}{2}$–2 hours.

Oxtail Soup

Tripe and Onions

Liver and Kidney

OFFAL BUT I LIKE YOU!

Really 'like' isn't quite the word. Offal is either loved or hated (how many lukewarm offal eaters do you know?). But I must be careful here: often it's indelicate promotion that is to blame. We're all seen those ghastly technicolour pictures in magazines that thrust the whole lot at us in its raw state. Ugh!

The word itself is scarcely a euphemism (Margaret Costa in her delightful *Four Seasons Cookbook* called it, pointedly, 'Awful Offal'). I frequently call it 'Spare Parts', because that's what it is—lots of nutritious bits and pieces full of potential and flavour. In Britain we've never really made the most of it because we've always had so much meat anyway. But now the time has come to learn from our French cousins, who have always had to make every bit of precious meat go as far as possible.

Fear not, I'm not about to offer you a Pig's Tail Ragout or some baked stuffed intestines. Instead I'm sticking to the more familiar and available liver and kidneys etc. which, although they are expensive, seem to go much further (so you need much less to make a meal). Once again, though, I do stress the seasons: English lamb's liver and kidney will be plentiful from June to October. From January to May imported lamb from places like New Zealand will be the best bet. Oxtails, ox kidney and liver will all be at their cheapest in the winter from about October; pork offal seems to be plentiful all the year round.

Braised Stuffed Hearts

(Serves 4–6)

6 lambs' hearts

For the stuffing:
3 tablespoons butter
1 small onion, peeled and finely chopped
2 oz (50 g) fresh white breadcrumbs
1 small cooking apple, peeled and chopped
Rind and juice of 1 orange
¼ teaspoon dried thyme
¼ teaspoon dried marjoram
3 tablespoons chopped parsley
Salt and freshly milled black pepper

Then you need:
Seasoned plain flour
1 tablespoon butter
1 tablespoon oil
1 large onion, peeled and chopped
¼ pint (150 ml) stock or water
¼ pint (150 ml) dry cider
2 teaspoons each butter and flour worked to a paste
1 teaspoon redcurrant jelly

Pre-heat the oven to mark 4/350°F/180°C

First wash the hearts thoroughly, and with a pair of scissors cut out all the tubes and the dividing wall in the centre of each heart (this is to make a neat pocket for the stuffing). Now prepare the stuffing by first heating the butter in a small saucepan and gently frying the onion until softened. Mix the onion and any fat in the pan with the remaining stuffing ingredients and season with salt and pepper. Now stuff the cavities in the hearts with the mixture and secure them at the top with small skewers. Roll the hearts in seasoned flour next, then brown in a casserole in the remaining butter and the oil. Stir in the chopped onion, cook this over a gentle heat until softened, then add the stock and cider. Bring to simmering point, cover and cook in the oven for about 2½–3 hours, or until the hearts are tender. When cooked, drain and arrange the hearts in a warmed serving dish. Bring the remaining pan juices to the boil and add small pieces of the butter and flour paste, stirring quickly. Then add the redcurrant jelly, taste and season. Pour the sauce over the hearts and serve.

Pork Kidneys with Mustard Cream Sauce

(Serves 4)

Pork kidneys soaked overnight have a much milder flavour and, as they're fairly reasonably priced, it's worth going to the trouble.

4 pork kidneys, soaked overnight in cold water
1 large onion, peeled and chopped
1 clove garlic, crushed
2 oz (50 g) lard
$\frac{1}{4}$ pint (150 ml) stock or hot water
$\frac{1}{4}$ pint (150 ml) dry cider
$1\frac{1}{2}$ teaspoons English mustard powder
$1\frac{1}{2}$ teaspoons genuine French mustard (Dijon)
A generous pinch thyme
2 tablespoons cream
1 teaspoon plain flour
A pinch cayenne pepper
Salt and freshly milled black pepper

First put the kettle on to boil, then after soaking the kidneys, slice them across into $\frac{1}{4}$-inch (5-mm) thick medallion-shaped slices and snip out the white cores using a pair of scissors. Now transfer them to a sieve and rinse them with a kettleful of boiling water; leave them to drain thoroughly and dry them in some kitchen paper. Next, in a cooking pot, melt the lard and soften the onion and garlic in it for 5 minutes. Then turn the heat up to high, add the drained and dried kidneys and brown them on all sides. Next lower the heat and stir in the flour to soak up the juices before adding the stock, cider, thyme and seasoning. Now put a lid on and simmer gently for 45 minutes. Meanwhile mix the mustards with the cream, add a pinch of cayenne pepper, then stir this into the cooked kidneys. Cook for a minute or two, then serve with buttered noodles (see page 160), or rice.

Spiced Kidneys in Yoghurt (Serves 2)

The imported frozen lambs' kidneys we get in the winter are never quite good enough to be served 'straight' but are perfectly good in a curry like this.

6 lambs' kidneys, skinned
2 tablespoons groundnut oil
2 medium-sized onions, peeled and thinly sliced
1 clove garlic, crushed
1 tablespoon tomato purée
2 teaspoons ground coriander
1 teaspoon turmeric
$\frac{1}{4}$ teaspoon cumin seeds
$\frac{1}{4}$ pint (150 ml) yoghurt
$\frac{1}{4}$ pint (150 ml) stock
Salt
About $\frac{1}{4}$ teaspoon chilli powder, or according to how hot you
   like it

To prepare the kidneys, halve them lengthways and snip out the cores using a sharp pair of kitchen scissors. Now heat the oil in a saucepan and fry the kidneys over a fairly high heat until lightly browned; then transfer them to a plate using a draining spoon. Next fry the sliced onion and garlic in the juices remaining in the pan until the onions are softened and golden. Then stir in the tomato purée, spices and yoghurt, and add the stock. Bring the sauce to simmering point, and continue to simmer very gently for about 15 minutes. Now taste it and flavour the sauce with salt and as much chilli powder as you want—but be careful, it is lethal if you add too much. Then return the kidneys (and any juices) to the pan, cover and simmer gently for 20 minutes. Taste again and season if it needs it. This is nice served with buttered noodles, and an extra dollop of yoghurt if available.

Kidney Stroganoff (Serves 4)

I think a Stroganoff made with lambs' kidneys is even nicer than one made with fillet steak.

12 lambs' kidneys
1 medium onion
2½ oz (60 g) butter
½ lb (225 g) mushrooms
A 5 fl oz (150 ml) carton soured cream
Salt and freshly milled black pepper
Freshly grated nutmeg

Begin by peeling the onion and slicing it into very thin rings. Now slice the rings in half and separate them to give you moon-shaped slivers. Melt 2 oz (50 g) of the butter in a large frying pan and gently soften the onion in it for 10 minutes. Meanwhile wipe the mushrooms, slice the stalks and caps thinly, then add them to the onion, stirring them around, and cook for a further 5 minutes. The kidneys should be first skinned and the cores snipped out and then cut into the thinnest slices possible. Turn the heat up a bit under the pan, add the kidney slices and brown them quickly, constantly turning the pieces over. Now turn the heat right down and stir in the soured cream, season with salt, pepper and nutmeg, and let everything simmer very gently for 5 minutes. Just before serving, stir in the remaining butter, then serve immediately with plain boiled rice.

Liver and Bacon Kebabs with Stuffing

(Serves 4)

I like to serve these with brown rice and a homemade tomato sauce.

$\frac{3}{4}$ lb (350 g) lambs' liver
About 6 rashers streaky bacon, rinded and cut in small squares
$1\frac{1}{2}$ oz (40 g) dripping or butter, melted

For the stuffing:
4 oz (110 g) fresh white breadcrumbs
2 oz (50 g) dripping or butter, melted
1 teaspoon grated onion
$\frac{1}{2}$ teaspoon mixed herbs
A pinch powdered mace
1 egg
Salt and freshly milled black pepper
About 2 tablespoons milk (to bind)

First cut the lambs' liver into bite-sized pieces, roughly all the same size. Then to make the stuffing, simply combine all the stuffing ingredients together in a bowl and mix thoroughly, with enough milk to bind. Next form the mixture into about 12 balls. Pierce one of them on to a flattened skewer, then thread the meats on (liver, bacon, liver, bacon, then another ball of stuffing and so on), filling 4 skewers. Now brush the kebabs liberally with melted dripping or butter and cook them under a fairly hot grill for about 10 minutes, turning and basting evenly at regular intervals. Serve hot, straight from the grill to the table.

Kidneys with Chipolatas (Serves 3)

A cheaper version, this one, of the famous Kidneys Turbigo.

6 lambs' kidneys, skinned, halved and cored
2 level tablespoons butter
2 tablespoons oil
3 slices bread, taken from a large white loaf
6 pork chipolata sausages
1 medium onion, peeled and chopped
½ pint (275 ml) stock
1 level teaspoon cornflour
1 level teaspoon mustard powder
1 teaspoon wine vinegar
½ teaspoon brown sugar
A couple of pinches cayenne pepper
Salt and freshly milled black pepper

First put a serving dish in a warm oven, then heat the butter
and oil in a frying pan, and fry the bread slices on both sides
until crisp and golden. Then drain the bread slices well on
kitchen paper and keep them hot in the oven. Next fry the
chipolatas, and keep these warm too. Then cook the kidneys
quickly for about 3–4 minutes and arrange them with the
chipolatas on the serving dish. Now fry the onion gently until
soft and golden and, using a draining spoon, arrange it over
the kidneys and sausages. Next add the stock to the pan and
boil briskly, scraping the base and sides of the pan, until the
stock is reduced by half. Now blend the cornflour, mustard
and vinegar in a small basin, stir into the stock, bring to the
boil and simmer for 2 or 3 minutes. Sprinkle in the sugar and a
couple of pinches of cayenne, taste to check the seasoning,
pour the sauce over the kidneys and sausages, and serve.

Liver and Vegetable Hotpot   (Serves 4)

1 lb of ox liver will be plenty for 4 people if you add some
bacon and vegetables and a thick crusty potato topping.

1 lb (450 g) ox liver
4 oz (110 g) streaky bacon rashers, rinded
1 carrot, scraped and cut in chunks
1 stick celery, cut in chunks
2 oz (50 g) swedes, peeled and cut in small chunks
1 tablespoon seasoned plain flour
3 largish onions, peeled and sliced
1 level teaspoon dried sage
Stock or water
1 teaspoon Worcestershire sauce
2 lb (900 g) potatoes, peeled and cut into thick slices
A little beef dripping, melted
Salt and freshly milled black pepper

Pre-heat the oven to mark 3/325°F/170°C

Cut the liver into slices about $\frac{1}{4}$ inch (5 mm) thick, then toss the
slices in some seasoned flour. Now in a casserole arrange the
slices of liver, cut vegetables, bacon and onions, seasoning
with pepper, salt and a little dried sage. When everything is in,
add enough stock or water to barely cover the liver etc.
(approximately 1–1$\frac{1}{4}$ pints/570–725 ml), add the Worcestershire sauce and cover everything with a thick layer of potatoes
overlapping each other. Now add a final sprinkling of salt and
pepper, cover closely and place the casserole in the oven for
about 1$\frac{1}{2}$ hours. Then take the lid off, brush the potatoes with a
little melted beef dripping and increase the heat to mark 6/
400°F/200°C to let them get brown and crusty on top—this
will take about another 30 minutes.

Liver with Crisp-fried Onions   (Serves 4)

Nothing is nicer with liver than some crispy deep-fried onions—and for this recipe, buy the liver from a helpful butcher who'll slice it very thinly for you.

1 lb (450 g) lambs' liver
Groundnut oil for deep-frying
2 oz (50 g) butter
2 tablespoons oil
Seasoned plain flour
2 medium onions, peeled and sliced in thin rings
Plain flour
1 large egg white
½ pint (275 ml) beef stock (or potato water)
Salt and freshly milled black pepper

The best way to do this is to heat the groundnut oil in a deep-fryer (to 350°F/180°C) and melt the butter and oil for the liver in a frying pan simultaneously, so that you can cook both the liver and the onions at more or less the same time. Also have some serving dishes keeping warm in the oven with some kitchen paper on them to absorb any excess oil. The liver slices should be coated in seasoned flour and fried quickly over a high heat in the butter and oil (about 1 minute on each side), then kept warm. The onions should be separated into thin rings, dipped first in plain flour, then in stiffly beaten egg white, and deep-fried till golden and crisp (for 1 or 2 minutes—it's best to do them a few at a time). Finally sprinkle 1 level tablespoon of plain flour into the pan juices left from the liver and cook it for a minute or two, then gradually stir in the stock to make a gravy, seasoning well with salt and pepper. Serve the liver garnished with the onions, and the gravy separately.

Kidney-stuffed Onions (Serves 4)

These are very good served with a very mild flavoured cheese sauce and some savoury rice.

4 large Spanish onions
6 lambs' kidneys, skinned and cored
2 oz (50 g) butter
2 teaspoons plain flour
4 tablespoons stock
A few drops Worcestershire sauce
$\frac{1}{4}$ teaspoon dried thyme
Salt and freshly milled pepper
A little extra butter

Peel the onions first, then parboil them in a covered pan with about 1 inch (2.5 cm) of water in it—give them about 40–45 minutes to half cook. Then drain them and leave them on one side till they are cool enough to handle. Now pre-heat the oven to mark 5/375°F/190°C, carefully remove the centres from the onions (keep them for soups or stews, etc.) and place the onions in a well-buttered gratin dish. Next chop the lambs' kidneys fairly small and fry them in 2 oz (50 g) of butter for about 5 minutes. Now stir in the flour, cook for a further minute or two and then gradually stir in the stock, a couple of drops of Worcestershire sauce and the thyme. Season well, simmer for a minute or two, then spoon the mixture into the hollowed onions. Add a small knob of butter to each onion and bake in the oven for 30–35 minutes, basting with the juices from time to time.

Oxtail Hotpot

(Serves 3)

1 oxtail, cut into joints
2–3oz (50–75 g) beef dripping
1 small turnip, peeled and cut into chunks
1 small swede, peeled and cut into chunks
2 medium carrots, scraped and cut into chunks
2 sticks celery, cut into chunks
3 small onions, peeled and left whole
1 lb (450 g) potatoes, peeled and cut into thick slices
1 pint (570 ml) hot water
2 teaspoons Worcestershire sauce
1 heaped tablespoon plain flour
$\frac{1}{2}$ teaspoon dried thyme
1 bayleaf
Salt and freshly milled black pepper
A little extra dripping (melted)

Pre-heat the oven to mark 2/300°F/150°C

In the largest frying pan you have, get the dripping really hot, and quickly brown the pieces of oxtail to a deep brown colour; then transfer them with a draining spoon to a large casserole, season them and sprinkle with thyme. Follow the oxtail with the vegetables (except the potatoes) browning these too just a little, and arrange them all around and over the pieces of oxtail. Add a little more pepper and salt and the bayleaf. Now stir the flour into the juices left in the frying pan and allow it to brown before gradually adding the hot water and the Worcestershire sauce. Then transfer the liquid to the casserole (sieving it if it's gone lumpy) and finally arrange the thickly sliced potatoes over the top. Put a lid on and bake for 3 hours, taking the lid off $\frac{1}{2}$ hour before the end, and finally brushing the potatoes with a little melted dripping and browning them until crisp under a hot grill for a few minutes before serving. This dish doesn't really need any extra vegetables to go with it.

Kidneys in Gravy
(Serves 2)

A very quick little casserole for 2 people that can be made in about 30 minutes from start to finish.

6 lambs' kidneys
2 oz (50 g) dripping or melted kidney fat
1 large onion, peeled and chopped
4 rashers unsmoked streaky bacon, rinded and chopped
¼ lb (110 g) dark flat mushrooms
1 dessertspoon plain flour
1 heaped teaspoon tomato purée
1 teaspoon Worcestershire sauce
½ pint (275 ml) hot water (or potato water)
Salt and freshly milled black pepper

Melt the fat in a large saucepan and soften the onion in it for 5 minutes; next add the chopped bacon, cook for another 5 minutes and then add the mushrooms and stir them around for a minute or two. Cut the kidneys into halves, pull off the skins and cut out all the white cores with a pair of scissors. Now turn the heat up under the saucepan, add the kidneys and brown them lightly, stirring them around a bit. Next sprinkle in the flour and stir to soak up the juices. Now stir the tomato purée and Worcestershire sauce into the hot water, then gradually add it to the pan, stirring as you do so. Season with salt and pepper, then put a lid on and simmer very gently for about 20 minutes. Serve with some creamy mashed potato.

Oxtail Braised in Cider   (Serves 4–6)

Alas, oxtail gets more expensive, but it's very plentiful in the autumn and needs some vegetables to eke it out.

2½–3 lb (1.1–1.35 kg) oxtail, cut into joints
Beef dripping
4 oz (110 g) streaky bacon, rinded and cut into cubes
3 large carrots, scraped and cut in thick chunks
2 large onions, peeled and sliced
1 oz (25 g) plain flour
¾ pint (425 ml) hot beef stock
¾ pint (425 ml) dry cider
½ teaspoon dried thyme
1 level teaspoon juniper berries, crushed
1 clove garlic, crushed
1 bayleaf
Salt and freshly milled black pepper
Some chopped fresh parsley as a garnish

Pre-heat the oven to mark 2/300°F/150°C

Start by melting the dripping in a large flameproof casserole, get it really hot, then brown the pieces of oxtail, 2 or 3 at a time. Remove them to a plate as they brown, then brown the bacon and chunks of carrot, and remove them to a plate as well. Next fry the onion till browned at the edges. Turn the heat down a bit, then stir in the flour to soak up the juices before gradually adding the stock and cider. Now return the meat, bacon and carrots to the casserole, add the thyme, juniper, garlic and bayleaf, and season with pepper and salt. Put a close-fitting lid on, transfer to the oven and cook for 3 hours. Just before serving, skim off any fat from the surface and sprinkle with fresh chopped parsley.

Liver Casserole   (Serves 6)

This is a recipe for summer when English lambs' liver is plentiful.

1¼lb (570 g) lambs' liver, cut into ¼-inch (5-mm) thick slices
Seasoned plain flour
1 oz (25 g) butter
1 tablespoon oil
2 medium onions, peeled and thinly sliced
½ lb (225 g) new carrots, washed and cut into 1-inch (2.5-cm)
   lengths
2 lb (900 g) small new potatoes, scraped
1 lb (450 g) tomatoes, skinned and sliced
½ pint (275 ml) stock
½ level teaspoon dried oregano
1 level tablespoon tomato purée
Salt and freshly milled black pepper

Pre-heat the oven to mark 4/350°F/180°C

Begin by drying the liver slices with some kitchen paper, then lightly coat the pieces in well-seasoned flour. Next heat the butter and oil together in a large frying pan and soften the sliced onion in it over a low heat for about 10 minutes. Now arrange half the floured liver slices in the base of a deep oven-proof casserole and cover with a layer of onion, carrots and scraped new potatoes, followed by half the sliced tomatoes. Then repeat all over again, finishing up with a layer of tomatoes. Combine the stock, oregano and tomato purée together in a jug, season, pour this into the casserole, cover closely and bake for approximately 1½ hours, or until the vegetables are tender.

Liver and Onion Yorkshire Pud (Serves 4)

If you think $\frac{1}{2}$ lb (225 g) lambs' liver might not be enough for 4 people, try this!

$\frac{1}{2}$ lb (225 g) lambs' liver
1 large onion, peeled and chopped
Some lard

For the batter:
1 egg
4 oz (110 g) plain flour
$\frac{1}{4}$ pint (150 ml) milk mixed with $\frac{1}{4}$ pint (150 ml) water
$\frac{1}{4}$ teaspoon fresh or dried thyme
Salt and freshly milled black pepper

Pre-heat the oven to mark 7/425°F/220°C

Place a thick-based meat roasting tin (measuring approximately 9 × 6$\frac{1}{2}$ inches/23 × 16 cm at the base) on a high shelf in the oven with about 1 oz (25 g) of lard in it. While it's heating through, make the batter by sifting the flour into a bowl, making a well in the centre of the flour, dropping the egg in and whisking it gradually, incorporating the flour and adding the milk-and-water mixture by degrees until you have a smooth batter. Season it with salt, freshly milled pepper and the thyme. Now cut the liver into thinnish strips about 1 inch (2.5 cm) in length. Fry the onion in a little more lard to soften (about 10 minutes), then add the liver and, with the heat fairly high, move it about and turn it to brown nicely—this should take around 2–3 minutes (be careful not to over-cook it). Now take the tin out of the oven, place it over a low heat on top of the stove to keep it sizzling, then spoon in the liver and onions and their juices, and pour the batter over. Return it to the oven and cook for about 35–40 minutes.

Faggots and Peas
(Serves 4)

A real old-fashioned favourite this one, full of flavour and not too expensive. Caul fat looks like lacy curtains and you can get it from a good butcher if you order it in advance.

1 lb (450 g) pig's liver, cut into 1-inch (2.5 cm) cubes
4 oz (110 g) green bacon, cut into 1-inch (2.5 cm) cubes
6 oz (175 g) pork back fat, cut into 1-inch (2.5 cm) cubes
2 medium onions, peeled
¾ pint (420 ml) stock
2 oz (50 g) fresh white breadcrumbs
¼ teaspoon dried thyme
¾ teaspoon dried sage
¼ teaspoon powdered mace
Salt and freshly milled pepper
A piece of caul fat, about 36 inches (90 cm) square

Then:
1 lb (450 g) green split peas
1¼ pints (725 ml) chicken stock
1 onion, peeled and quartered
2 oz (50 g) butter

Pre-heat the oven to mark 4/350°F/180°C

First place the liver, bacon, back fat and onions in a casserole and pour in the stock. Bake this for 45 minutes, then pour the contents of the casserole into a large sieve set over a bowl. Now mince the cooked meats through the fine blade of the mincer, and mix them with the breadcrumbs, herbs and spice. Then season well with salt and pepper and form the mixture into six little cake shapes. Next rinse the caul fat in a bowl of warm water, drain well and spread it out carefully. Cut out 6 × 6-inch (15 cm) squares, wrap the faggots in them and pack together in a greased baking dish just big enough to hold them. Now skim the fat from the stock and pour ½ pint (275 ml) of the stock over the faggots in the baking dish and bake (uncovered) for about 45 minutes. To cook the peas, put the chicken stock and quartered onion into a pan and bring to the boil. Add the split peas to the pan and bring back to the boil, turn down the heat, then cover and simmer very gently for $1\frac{1}{2}$ hours or until the peas are tender. Then mash with the butter and add salt and pepper to taste (if the mixture is a little dry, add some of the remaining stock from the faggot recipe). Serve the peas with the faggots and the juices poured over.

BANGERS are BEAUTIFUL

Almost every country in the world has some sort of national sausage. I've seen them threaded on skewers over glowing charcoal on the streets of Istanbul and simmering in garlic-laced bean pots in the Tuscan hills, while in France there are dozens of varieties, from the spicy coarse-cut saucissons of Provence to the pale, gutsy andouillettes of the Lyonnais.

In Britain we have bangers. They burst and spread them-selves out over the pan, amalgamating with each other before charring, crisp and black outside and pink and soft within.

Well, they say it takes all sorts, but my complaint is that we really don't have enough sorts: the bran-filled monster I've just described gets awfully boring. Fortunately, we do have a *few* 'beautiful' bangers, made by butchers up and down the country who take a pride in their own particular recipe (my own butcher's are excellent). And if you haven't got a butcher who makes good ones, I suggest you try to get hold of some from better supermarkets.

Good sausages, it's true, are more expensive but, because they contain more meat, they don't shrivel and shrink in the cooking, releasing floods of watery fat. Having hunted down the perfect banger, these recipes offered here will help to make them go a bit further (or, if you're prepared to do without skins, you can even make your own).

Homemade Sausages (Serves 3)

1 lb (450 g) minced pork (a cheaper cut, finely minced)
2 oz (50 g) shredded beef suet
½ small onion, peeled and grated
2 thick slices bread from a large loaf (crusts off)
1½ tablespoons milk
3 fresh sage leaves, chopped small (or ¼ teaspoon dried)
¼ whole nutmeg, grated
¼ teaspoon chopped thyme (fresh or dried)
1½ tablespoons seasoned plain flour
Lard
Salt and freshly milled black pepper

Take a large bowl and mix the meat and suet together very thoroughly, then add the grated onion. Soak the bread in the milk, squeeze the excess liquid out, and pop that in too; then mix very thoroughly. Now add the sage, nutmeg, thyme and a good seasoning of salt and freshly milled black pepper. Take care to give it a thorough mixing—it's most important. Next take about a tablespoon of the mixture, press it together, roll it into a sausage shape on a clean surface, then roll it in seasoned flour—and carry on like that until all your sausages are made. To cook, fry them in hot lard to brown all round, then reduce the heat to medium to cook them through. They take about 25 minutes in all. Drain them on crumpled kitchen paper and serve with sauté potatoes and a crisp salad, or with creamy mashed potato, mustard or chutney.

Sausages with Chilli Sauce

(Serves 3)

1 lb (450 g) pork sausages
1 whole fresh red chilli (or $\frac{1}{4}$ teaspoon chilli powder)
1 tablespoon olive oil
1 onion, peeled and chopped
1 small green pepper, de-seeded and diced
2 cloves garlic, crushed
A 14 oz (400 g) tin Italian tomatoes
1 teaspoon dried basil
$\frac{1}{4}$ teaspoon sugar
1 teaspoon tomato purée
Salt and freshly milled black pepper

Begin by de-seeding the chilli (if you are using a whole one), discarding the fiery seeds and chopping the red part finely. Now heat the olive oil in a flameproof casserole or saucepan, brown the sausages all round and, using a draining spoon, remove them from the pan. Next stir the onion, green pepper and garlic into the fat remaining in the pan and cook gently until softened (about 10 minutes). Now stir in the remaining ingredients, bring up to simmering point, then return the sausages to the pan. Allow it to simmer very gently (uncovered), stirring occasionally, for about 25 minutes until the tomatoes are reduced to a thick sauce-like consistency. Then taste and season with salt and pepper before serving. This is very good served with buttered noodles or creamy mashed potato.

Sausage-stuffed Onions

(Serves 4)

If you can, try to get the very largest (preferably Spanish) onions for this.

4 large Spanish onions
$\frac{1}{2}$ lb (225 g) good sausagemeat
2 oz (50 g) mushrooms, finely chopped
$1\frac{1}{2}$ oz (40 g) butter

$\frac{1}{2}$ teaspoon dried sage
1 oz (25 g) dry white breadcrumbs
2 tablespoons chopped fresh parsley
A 5 fl oz (150 ml) carton yoghurt
1 small cooking apple, peeled, cored and chopped
1 clove garlic, crushed
Paprika
Salt and freshly milled black pepper
A little extra butter

Pre-heat the oven to mark 6/400°F/200°C

After you've peeled the onions, put them in a large pan of boiling salted water. Bring the water back to the boil, cover and simmer gently for about 30 minutes. Then drain the onions and leave them to cool. Now cut a thin cap from the top of each onion and scoop out the centres, leaving a fairly substantial shell. Arrange the onion cases (packing them closely together) in a deep, buttered baking dish. Then chop up the onion you removed. Next heat $1\frac{1}{2}$ oz (40 g) of butter in a frying pan and measure 3 tablespoons of the chopped onion into it. Fry briskly for a minute or two before adding the sausagemeat and sage—mashing it down with a fork until separate and evenly coloured. Then stir in the garlic, mushrooms, breadcrumbs and apple. Taste and season with salt and pepper (some sausagemeats come quite highly seasoned to start with, so do taste it first). Now remove the pan from the heat and stir in a tablespoon of yoghurt together with the parsley. Put the mixture into the onion shells—if it seems a little too much, just pile it up on top. Then transfer the baking dish to the top half of the oven and bake for 20 minutes. Finally put a blob of yoghurt on each onion and dust with paprika. Replace in the oven for a further 5–10 minutes and serve with creamy mashed potato.

Note: Any bits of onion centres left over can be used for soups or stocks.

Frankfurters with Hot Potato Salad   (Serves 4)

If you have a delicatessen in your area, try to get the really long frankfurters for this recipe, as they're generally much better than the supermarket variety.

8 large frankfurters
1½ lb (700 g) potatoes
1 medium onion, peeled, halved and thinly sliced
6 tablespoons oil
2 tablespoons cider vinegar
1 teaspoon made mustard
A few drops Tabasco sauce
2 tablespoons chopped fresh parsley
1 clove garlic, crushed
Salt and freshly milled black pepper

To start with, scrub the potatoes well (but don't peel them), then boil them in salted water until they're just tender. While that's happening, heat 2 tablespoons of oil in a separate pan and fry the onion and crushed garlic for 2 or 3 minutes. Then add the remaining oil and the cider vinegar, stir in the mustard, Tabasco, salt and freshly milled pepper, and heat until boiling. Then turn the heat low and, at this stage, poach the frankfurters (but check with the supplier for how long, because it does vary). Next drain the boiled potatoes, put them in a warm serving bowl and pour over the hot oil and vinegar mixture. Now sprinkle with the parsley and, using a sharp knife, roughly chop the potatoes. Then serve with the hot cooked frankfurters on top, and have some extra mustard on the table.

Note: I always like to leave the skins on the potatoes, but if you like you can peel them off as soon as the potatoes are drained.

Bangers Braised in Cider
(Serves 3)

I always use herb-flavoured sausages for this, but any sort of pork sausages will do.

1 lb (450 g) pork sausages
Lard
$\frac{1}{2}$ lb (225 g) lean streaky bacon in one piece (then cut into cubes)
$\frac{1}{2}$ lb (225 g) small button onions, peeled
1 heaped teaspoon plain flour
$\frac{1}{2}$ pint (275 ml) dry cider
1 clove garlic, crushed
1 bayleaf
$\frac{1}{2}$ teaspoon dried thyme
Salt and freshly milled black pepper
1 Cox's apple, cored and cut into rings (no need to peel it)
A little butter

Pre-heat the oven to mark 4/350°F/180°C

Take a large flameproof casserole, melt a little lard in it and brown the sausages all round. Then, using a slotted spoon, remove them to a plate whilst you brown the bacon cubes and onions lightly. When they're done, sprinkle in the flour to soak up the juices, then gradually stir in the cider. Now pop the sausages back in, plus the garlic, bayleaf and thyme and a little seasoning; put a lid on when it all comes to simmering point and then transfer to the oven for 30 minutes. When the 30 minutes is up, remove the lid and cook for a further 20–30 minutes. Before serving, fry the apple rings in butter until soft and garnish the casserole with them. This is lovely served with spicy red cabbage.

Toad-in-the-Hole with Sage and Onions

(Serves 4)

Not an attractive name, admittedly, but it's a delicious classic, especially if you make it with good-quality pork sausages, a little sage and fried onion rings.

1 lb (450g) pure pork sausages
Beef dripping or lard
2 medium onions, peeled and sliced thinly
6 oz (175g) plain flour
2 large eggs
6 fl oz (175 ml) milk
4 fl oz (110 ml) water
Salt and freshly milled black pepper
1 level teaspoon dried sage

Pre-heat the oven to mark 7/425°F/220°C

First put a tablespoon of dripping into a solid-based roasting tin (base measuring about 9 × 7 inches (23 × 18cm)) and pop it into the oven to heat. Then in a frying pan melt some more fat and brown the onions for about 5 minutes or so until they have softened a bit. Remove them to a plate and lightly brown the sausages all round—again for about 5 minutes. While they're browning, make the batter by sifting the flour into a bowl. Make a well in the middle, drop the eggs in and, using an electric hand-whisk (or a fork), whisk the eggs, incorporating the flour and adding the milk and water mixed together first. Season the batter with salt, pepper and sage. When the fat in the tin starts to sizzle, take it out of the oven and keep it sizzling by placing it on top of the stove over a medium heat. Then put in the sausages and the onions on top of them and, making sure the fat is still very hot, pour in the batter. Quickly shake the tin to get the batter all round the base of the sausages etc., then transfer the tin back to the highest shelf of the oven and let it bake for about 40 minutes, or until puffy and crisp. Serve straightaway, with gravy or apple and onion sauce.

Sausages with Lentils (Serves 4)

1½ lb (700 g) sausages
6 oz (175 g) dried green lentils (not the orange ones)
1 large onion, peeled and chopped
2 cloves garlic, crushed
1 level tablespoon butter
1 tablespoon oil
14oz (400 g) can Italian tomatoes
1 level teaspoon sugar
2 or 3 pinches dried thyme
1 bayleaf
Salt and freshly milled black pepper

Rinse the lentils, place them in a saucepan with enough water
to cover (don't add any salt), bring them to simmering point
and simmer gently for about 30 minutes, or until the lentils are
tender but not disintegrating. Now drain them, and keep the
cooking liquid. Then fry the onion and garlic in the butter and
oil, add the tinned tomatoes, sugar, thyme and bayleaf, and let
it all simmer gently (without a lid) until the liquid reduces and
it becomes rather thick—you may need to stir it now and then.
Now in a frying pan brown the sausages all over in a little more
oil. Then, using a draining spoon, transfer them to the tomato
mixture. Add the lentils now and approximately ½ pint (275
ml) of the liquid they were cooked in. Stir well, then continue
cooking over a very gentle heat for about 30 minutes—again
without a lid, and if the mixture begins to look dry add a little
more liquid. Taste and add pepper and salt, if it needs it,
before serving.

Pork Sausages with Cider Sauce   (Serves 3)

I first made this using red wine, but now I've switched to cider and it's every bit as good.

1 lb (450 g) good-quality pork sausages
1 oz (25 g) lard
1 onion, peeled and chopped
4 slices streaky bacon, rinded and chopped
2 level teaspoons plain flour
4 oz (110 g) dark mushrooms, sliced
4 fl oz (110 ml) dry cider
$\frac{1}{4}$ pint (150 ml) stock or water
2 teaspoons tomato purée
$\frac{1}{4}$ teaspoon dried thyme
1 teaspoon redcurrant jelly
Salt and freshly milled black pepper

First gently brown the sausages all over in the lard, then using a draining spoon transfer them to a plate and keep them on one side. Now add the onion and the bacon to the fat remaining in the pan and cook these for about 10 minutes, or until the onion is soft. Then sprinkle in the flour and stir it round to soak up the juices; add the mushrooms and cook for 5 more minutes before stirring in the cider and stock. Next add the tomato purée, thyme and redcurrant jelly, bring to simmering point, taste and season and cook gently without a cover for about 15 minutes. These are delicious served with some creamy mashed potatoes or even some onion-flavoured rice (see page 157).

Sausages Boulangère (Serves 3)

These are nice served with some freshly made sharp English mustard.

1 lb (450 g) sausages
1½ lb (700 g) potatoes, peeled and very thinly sliced
1 medium onion, peeled and finely chopped
¼ pint (150 ml) milk
¼ pint (150 ml) stock or water
A little oil
1 teaspoon dried mixed herbs
1 oz (25 g) butter
Salt and freshly milled black pepper

Pre-heat the oven to mark 4/350°F/180°C

Brown the sausages all over in a little oil in a frying pan—this should take around 5 or 6 minutes—and while that's happening put a smear of butter round the base of a casserole. Then put in a layer of the potatoes, a sprinkling of onion and seasoning, and repeat the layers until all the potatoes are in, finishing off with a few flecks of butter. Now remove the browned sausages from the pan, using a draining spoon, and place these on top of the potatoes. Sprinkle in the dried herbs, pour in the milk and water, cover the casserole with a piece of foil, place it in the oven and bake for about 45 minutes. Then remove the foil and bake for a further 15–20 minutes, or until the potatoes are tender when tested with a thin skewer.

Purée of Peas with Sausages   (Serves 3)

This makes a nice accompaniment to 1 lb (450 g) of ordinary fried sausages.

1 lb (450 g) sausages, fried
1 lb (450 g) green split peas
1 small onion, peeled and stuck with 4 cloves
¼ teaspoon mixed herbs
4 tablespoons cream
1 oz (25 g) butter
Salt and freshly milled black pepper
Freshly grated nutmeg

Put the split peas in a pan and cover them with cold water. Bring this to the boil very slowly, remove from the heat and leave to soak for 1 hour. Then drain the peas and place them back in the saucepan together with the onion stuck with cloves, the mixed herbs and some salt. Cover again with cold water and simmer till tender (about 20 minutes). Then drain the peas again and rub them through a sieve into the top of a double saucepan (or a basin sitting over some simmering water); stir in the cream and butter, and leave it like this for about 20 minutes, stirring now and then until it becomes very thick. Season with pepper and freshly grated nutmeg, and more salt if it needs it. Serve the purée piled on to a plate with the fried sausages on top.

Poor Man's Cassoulet
(Serves 4)

This is a much cheaper and easier version than the original
classic Cassoulet. Nevertheless, do try to get decent bangers if
possible.

1 lb (450 g) pork sausages
¾ lb (350 g) long haricot beans
Groundnut oil
½ lb (225 g) streaky bacon, bought in one piece then cut into
   cubes
3 medium onions, peeled and sliced
3 cloves garlic, finely chopped
1½ tablespoons tomato purée
¾ level teaspoon dried thyme
4 oz (110 g) fresh white breadcrumbs
Salt and freshly milled black pepper

Pre-heat the oven to mark 1/275°F/140°C

Either soak the beans overnight or wash them, place them in a
saucepan, cover with plenty of cold water, bring to the boil and
let them boil for 1 minute. Then turn out the heat and let them
soak for 2–3 hours. Then in a flameproof casserole, heat some
oil and brown the sausages to a nice golden colour. Remove
them to a plate, then colour the bacon cubes a little and transfer
them to join the waiting sausages. Now in the juices left in the
pan soften the onion and garlic for 10 minutes, and while that's
happening drain the beans (reserving their soaking water). Put a
layer of beans into the cooking pot containing the onion and
garlic, then add half the sausages and bacon, followed by more
beans, the rest of the sausages and bacon, and finally the rest of
the beans. Next measure 1¼ pints (725 ml) of the soaking water,
stir 1½ tablespoons of tomato purée into it along with the thyme
and a seasoning of salt and pepper—but be sparing with the salt
(because of the bacon). Pour this over the rest of the ingredients, then cover and bake for 2 hours. Then take the lid off,
sprinkle the breadcrumbs all over the top, and bake (without a
lid) for a further hour. This is very rich and hefty, so a green
salad is really all it needs to go with it.

COOK FOR VICTORY

1976 must surely go down as the year Britain took to the spade.
Was it the potato crisis, the exorbitant prices or the media
jumping on another bandwagon? Where once the bookshelves

were dominated by cookery books, there are now an equal number of baffling and bewildering gardening books and step-by-step part-works with titles like *Grow It and Cook It, Grow It and Freeze It*.

Very commendable, and I hope the harvest proved worth all the sweat, because for too long (while meat was plentiful) vegetables have played a secondary role, just a little something to help the meat go down. I believe this is changing now, if only because we've travelled abroad more and been made more aware of the full potential of vegetables—that what might have been a simple uninspiring meal can be transformed into something much more special by the clever treatment of vegetables.

Take marrow, one of our cheapest and most easily grown vegetables, yet so often relegated to a watery white sauce. Try it on its own with tomatoes, garlic and crushed coriander seeds, and see what I mean. If you grow fresh herbs, then do make some herb butter (by chopping up a mixture of herbs and combining them with butter) and just swirl a knob of this around cooked new potatoes or carrots or cauliflower—it instantly puts them into the four-star bracket. All the recipes here attempt to make the most of vegetables, whether they're to be eaten on their own or used to jazz up cold meat, sausages or other fairly simple dishes.

Broad Bean Salad

(Serves 2)

1½ lb (700 g) broad beans (that is, 1½ lb/700 g before shelling)
1 rasher lean bacon, rinded
1 tablespoon fresh chopped herbs (I use a mixture of tarragon,
   marjoram and parsley)
4 spring onions, finely chopped
crisp lettuce leaves

For the vinaigrette dressing:
1 level teaspoon crushed rock salt
1 dessertspoon lemon juice
1 dessertspoon wine vinegar
½ clove garlic, crushed
1 teaspoon English mustard powder
4 dessertspoons oil
Freshly milled black pepper

First cook the bacon until it's really crisp, then drain it well and crumble it into very small pieces. Next make the dressing by dissolving the salt in the lemon juice and vinegar for ½ hour, then shake it with the rest of the ingredients in a screw-top jar to get everything thoroughly amalgamated. Now cook the shelled beans in a very little salted water for about 5 minutes—it's very important not to overcook them or they'll lose their colour and go mushy—then drain them thoroughly and toss them in the dressing while they're still warm. When they're cool, toss in the herbs, finely chopped spring onion and bacon, and serve the salad on some crisp lettuce leaves.

Baked Aubergines

(Serves 4)

Aubergines done like this go extremely well with lamb, or they're good on their own as a lunch-time dish with lots of fresh bread and perhaps a green salad.

4 aubergines (about 1¾ lb/800 g)
4 tablespoons oil
1 large onion, peeled and finely chopped
6 fairly large tomatoes, skinned and chopped
2 cloves garlic, crushed
2 tablespoons finely chopped fresh parsley
A very generous pinch each ground allspice, powdered cinnamon and caster sugar
Salt and freshly milled black pepper
A little butter

For the topping:
2–3 tablespoons dry white breadcrumbs
1 tablespoon grated Parmesan or other cheese
1 tablespoon butter

First cut the aubergines into smallish pieces, then place them in a colander and sprinkle with 2 heaped teaspoons of salt. Put a plate on top of them with a weight on it and leave them to drain for an hour. Then, when you're ready to cook them, pre-heat the oven to mark 5/375°F/190°C and well butter a shallow baking dish. Drain and dry the aubergines as thoroughly as possible on kitchen paper, then heat the oil in a frying pan. When it's hot, add the aubergines to the pan and fry them until they're a pale golden colour. Now add the onion to the pan and continue cooking until it has softened slightly; then add the prepared tomatoes, crushed garlic and parsley, and season with the spices, caster sugar, salt and pepper. Simmer gently now, stirring a bit, for about 5 minutes. Next transfer the mixture to the baking dish, sprinkle the top with a mixture of cheese and breadcrumbs, and dot the surface with the butter. Then bake near the top of the oven for about 30 minutes, or until bubbling and browned on top.

Tomato and Chilli Sauce

(Serves 2)

$\frac{3}{4}$ lb (350 g) red, ripe tomatoes, skinned
1 small onion, peeled and finely chopped
1 clove garlic, crushed
1 tablespoon olive oil
1 teaspoon tomato purée
1 teaspoon dried basil
$\frac{1}{4}$ teaspoon chilli powder
1 tablespoon olive oil
Salt and freshly milled black pepper

To skin the tomatoes, pour boiling water over them, leave for 1 minute, then put them in cold water and slip the skins off. Now halve them and chop the flesh quite small. Next soften the onion and garlic in a saucepan with the olive oil, then add the tomatoes, tomato purée, the basil and chilli powder, and season with salt. Stir well, simmer gently for 15 minutes with the lid on and then for a further 10 or 15 minutes without the lid. When it's ready, taste to check the seasoning, then either sieve the mixture or blend it in a liquidiser, or else serve it just as it is.

White Cabbage with Garlic and Coriander (Serves 4)

Cooking vegetables in the oven is only economical if the oven is on anyway, so try to cook this dish when you are using the oven for something else.

1 small white cabbage, weighing about 1½ lb (700 g)
2 tablespoons groundnut oil
1 large clove garlic, crushed
1 heaped teaspoon coriander seeds
Salt and freshly milled black pepper

First take away any stale or tough outer leaves from the cabbage, then using a sharp knife cut it into quarters and remove the tough stalky bits. Now, leaving the quarters intact, wash them and then dry them as thoroughly as possible. Pour the oil over the base of the casserole, add the crushed garlic and put it into the oven to heat through—the temperature should be mark 4/350°F/180°C. Meanwhile crush the coriander seeds, preferably in a pestle and mortar but failing that you can use a small basin and the end of a rolling pin. When the oil is hot and beginning to sizzle, add the crushed coriander seeds, then the pieces of cabbage. Baste each piece a little, season with salt and pepper, put a lid on the casserole and put it back in the oven for about 40 minutes, or until the cabbage is tender when tested with a skewer.

Turnips Boulangère (Serves 6)

Potatoes Boulangère are quite well known, but in fact this method works particularly well with turnips too.

2 lb (900 g) small (tender) turnips
1 onion, peeled and finely chopped
2 slices streaky bacon, rinded and chopped small
¼ pint (150 ml) hot stock
¼ pint (150 ml) milk

1 oz (25 g) of butter
Some extra butter
Salt and freshly milled black pepper

Pre-heat the oven to mark 4/350°F/180°C

First peel the turnips and slice them as thinly as possible. Then arrange the ingredients in a 4½-pint (2.5-litre) casserole or baking dish (generously buttered) as follows: a layer of sliced turnips in the base, followed by a sprinkling of onion and a seasoning of salt and pepper. Continue with another layer of turnips, then onion and so on until everything is in and you've finished up with a layer of turnips on top. Now pour in the milk and hot stock, season once again, and dot the surface with the 1 oz (25 g) of butter. Finally, sprinkle the chopped bacon over the top and cover it all with a sheet of buttered foil. Bake in the top half of the oven for an hour. After that time remove the foil, and bake for a further 30 minutes—or until the turnips feel soft when tested with a skewer.

Mashed Swede with Bacon   (Serves 6)

2 lb (900 g) swedes
4 rashers streaky bacon, rinded and chopped small
2 oz (50 g) butter
2 tablespoons milk
Salt and freshly milled black pepper

Peel the swedes, cut them into smallish cubes, place them in a saucepan and pour over enough boiling water to just cover them. Add some salt and simmer for about 20–30 minutes, or until the cubes are tender. Now pour the swede into a colander to drain thoroughly and return the saucepan to the heat, add a knob of butter and then quickly fry the chopped bacon until it's just beginning to crisp. Next return the swede to the saucepan and mash to a creamy pulp, adding the rest of the butter and the milk. Season well with salt and freshly milled black pepper, and serve piled on to a warm serving dish.

Courgettes à la Grecque   (Serves 2)

If you decide to grow courgettes they'll come at you at such a rate that you'll be wondering what on earth to do with them next. So here's an idea.

$\frac{3}{4}$ lb (350 g) small courgettes
3 tablespoons oil (preferably olive)
1 medium-sized onion, peeled and chopped small
1 clove garlic, crushed
1 tablespoon wine vinegar
6 tablespoons water
6 coriander seeds, lightly crushed
6 black peppercorns, lightly crushed
$\frac{1}{2}$ teaspoon oregano
Juice of 1 small lemon
Salt
1 large tomato, skinned and chopped
1 tablespoon chopped fresh parsley

First heat 2 tablespoons of the oil in a heavy pan and soften the onion and garlic in it gently for about 10 minutes. Then add the wine vinegar, the water, the crushed coriander and peppercorns, oregano, the lemon juice and a little salt. Bring to the boil and simmer for 5 minutes. Then prepare the courgettes: don't peel them, just wipe them, trim off the ends and cut into 1-inch (2.5-cm) slices. Add them to the sauce together with the chopped tomato, stir, put the lid on and simmer over a gentle heat for about 20 minutes, or until they're tender. Now transfer the lot to a serving dish, allow to cool, then cover and chill. Just before serving sprinkle with the remaining tablespoon of oil and some fresh chopped parsley. Then all it needs is some crusty fresh bread.

Purée of Parsnips

(Serves 4)

If you make this in January or February, when parsnips are really cheap, then I think a ¼ pint (150 ml) of cream will be justified.

1 lb (450 g) parsnips
¾ pint (420 ml) hot water
¼ pint (150 ml) single cream
Freshly grated nutmeg
Salt and freshly milled black pepper

First peel the parsnips, discard any of the woody centre bits and chop them up into small cubes. Now bring the water up to boiling point in a saucepan, add the cubed parsnips, bring them back to simmering point, cover and cook for about 10 minutes, or until tender. Then drain them, reserving their cooking liquid. Next, either tip them into a liquidiser and blend them to a purée with the cream or sieve them, beating the cream in with a fork bit by bit. Either way, taste and season with freshly grated nutmeg, salt and pepper, adding 1 or 2 tablespoons of their cooking liquid, if you think it needs it.

Marrow with Tomatoes and Coriander (Serves 4)

A 1½-lb (700-g) marrow (a young one will be smallish, have a
shiny skin, and when you press one of the ridges with your
thumb it will leave an impression)
½ lb (225 g) red ripe tomatoes (about 4 medium), skinned and
chopped
½ medium onion, peeled and chopped
1 clove garlic, crushed
¾ teaspoon coriander seeds, crushed
1 dessertspoon fresh chopped basil (or 1 level teaspoon dried)
1 tablespoon oil
Salt and freshly milled black pepper

Pre-heat the oven to mark 3/325°F/170°C

In a flameproof casserole melt the oil, add the onion and
crushed garlic, and soften for about 5 minutes; then stir in the
chopped tomatoes and cook for a further 5 minutes. If the
marrow is fresh it won't need peeling; simply cut it into rough
1½-inch (4-cm) chunks and add them to the tomatoes and
onions along with the coriander seeds (crushed first with a
pestle and mortar or with the back of a tablespoon). Then add
the basil, and season with salt and pepper. Stir everything
around well, put a lid on and place the casserole in the oven to
cook for about 1 hour. About 10 minutes before the end of the
cooking time, put the casserole back on the top of the stove
and simmer without a lid to reduce some of the liquid.

Note: This tastes good even cold or re-heated the next day.

New Potatoes with Bacon and Onion

(Serves 3)

Serve this with fresh fried eggs and you have a very quick and simple supper dish.

1½ lb (700 g) new potatoes, scrubbed but not peeled
1 oz (25 g) butter
1 tablespoon oil
6 slices bacon, rinded and cut into strips
1 large onion, peeled and chopped small
1 clove garlic, crushed
Salt and freshly milled black pepper

First of all slice the potatoes into rounds no more than about ¼ inch (5 mm) thick. Then melt the butter and oil in a large heavy frying pan, and fry the bacon strips, chopped onion and crushed garlic over a gentle heat until just softened. Now add the sliced potatoes to the pan, season with salt and freshly milled black pepper, give it all a really good stir around, then cover with a well-fitting lid (a heatproof plate will do if you've no lid) and leave to cook very gently for about 20–25 minutes, or until the potato slices are tender. Stir once or twice during the cooking to make sure that the heat is not too high and that the potatoes are not sticking to the base of the pan. When they're ready, spoon them into a heatproof serving dish and serve with fried eggs on top.

Soufflé'd Jacket Potatoes (Serves 4)

4 large potatoes baked in their jackets
2 oz (50 g) butter
6–8 spring onions, finely chopped
A 5-fl oz (150-ml) carton soured cream or yoghurt
3 eggs, separated
Salt and freshly milled black pepper
1 tablespoon chopped parsley

Pre-heat the oven to mark 6/400°F/200°C

Bake the potatoes. Then as soon as they're cooked, remove them from the oven, leaving the heat at mark 6/400°F/200°C, then (with your hands in oven gloves, or using a teacloth for protection), cut the potatoes in half and scoop out the centres into a bowl. Next arrange the potato shells in a shallow roasting tin (using one potato to prop up another if they don't sit comfortably straight). Now melt the butter in a saucepan and fry the spring onions for 2–3 minutes; then add all the onion and melted butter to the potato together with the soured cream and egg yolks, and whisk (preferably with an electric hand-whisk) until smooth. Taste and season well with salt and pepper and add the parsley. Now, with a clean whisk, beat the egg whites until stiff and carefully fold them into the potato mixture. Pile the mixture back into the potato shells and return them to the top half of the oven for 15–20 minutes, or until puffed and golden brown on top. Serve immediately—with some homemade chutney to dip the skins in.

Irish Potatoes

This is an excellent way to jazz up potatoes, especially for serving with cold leftover meat.

2 lb (900 g) potatoes
½ lb (225 g) green cabbage, shredded
1 bunch spring onions, chopped
2 oz (50 g) butter, meat dripping or bacon fat
2 tablespoons cream (or top of the milk)
Salt and freshly milled black pepper

Put a kettle on to boil while you peel the potatoes and cut them into even-sized pieces. Then place them in a saucepan, add salt, pour over enough boiling water to just cover them, and simmer until tender. Meanwhile place the washed cabbage in a saucepan, add salt and pour boiling water on that too. When it comes to the boil, cook it for 5 minutes, then drain very thoroughly in a colander, pressing out all the excess liquid very carefully. Now return the saucepan to the heat, melt the fat in it and add the spring onions and drained cabbage. Stir them around, keeping the heat very low. Then put a lid on and let them sweat gently without browning for 10 minutes. While that's happening, drain the potatoes, add some pepper and whip them to a purée with the cream or milk (an electric hand-whisk will do this in seconds). Now add the onion and cabbage and their juices, combine them with the potato and serve very hot.

Old-fashioned Bubble and Squeak (Serves 2)

It's funny how some very humble dishes like this one can be very special simply because of their rarity—so here's to a comeback for good old Bubble and Squeak!

1 lb (450 g) potatoes, peeled
1 small cabbage
1 heaped tablespoon well-seasoned plain flour
1 oz (25 g) butter
Salt and freshly milled black pepper
Some good beef dripping for frying

Put the potatoes on to cook in some salted boiling water, then half fill a medium-sized saucepan with some more salted water and bring it to the boil. Cut the cabbage into quarters, remove the hard stalk and shred the rest. Wash it thoroughly, then plunge it into the fast-boiling water, put a lid on and let it boil for about 6 minutes. Now pour it into a colander, put a plate (one that fits inside the colander) on top of the cabbage, place a weight on top and leave it to drain very thoroughly. When the potatoes are cooked, add some pepper and the butter. Mash them (with an electric hand-mixer if you have one) until smooth—don't add any milk, though, because you don't want them to be too soft. Now mix the well-drained cabbage into the potato, and when it is cool take tablespoons of the mixture and shape them into round cakes, which should then be dusted in the seasoned flour. Fry them in hot dripping to a good, crisp, golden brown on both sides. Drain on crumpled greaseproof paper and serve immediately.

Note: You can, of course, make this with leftover potatoes and cabbage or sprouts; also a little chopped fried onion is a nice addition.

GO WITH THE GRAIN

It is a fact of life—established by the charts and graphs of the British Nutrition Foundation—that as our affluence increases, so our cereal consumption decreases. And the same is true in reverse, of course. But whatever our economic condition, grains in all their forms are obviously very important (one need hardly mention that they are the staple food of two-thirds of the world).

I've always had great admiration for the way the Italians, for instance, manage to stretch out their meagre meat rations with the most delicate dishes of pasta. In fact, our household is hooked on it, and we have it regularly once a week. I have investigated *making* pasta at home, but it is quite a strenuous and lengthy exercise and, at the time of writing, doesn't seem to me all that much of a saving (so I haven't included it here). But bear in mind, when you're buying pasta, that a pound (450 g) of it serves 4 people—so it really is economical.

Some people still feel nervous about cooking rice. However, if you follow the instructions I've given here, you won't ever have any trouble. Don't, whatever you do, buy the so-called 'easy-cook' rice. It's much more expensive, and as all rice is easy to cook once it has been explained, you'll have wasted your money!

Onion Rice

Cooking rice needn't be a problem if a few simple rules are followed. The first rule is always buy good-quality long-grain rice; the second is it's better to measure rice and liquid by volume rather than by weight; and, most important of all, don't keep opening the cooking pot and giving the rice hefty stirs, because this will break the grains, release the starch and cause the rice to become soggy. Don't stir it at all during the cooking, just wait until all the liquid has been absorbed, then tip the rice into a serving dish and fluff it *gently* with a fork.

1 teacup long-grain rice
1 oz (25 g) butter
1 tablespoon groundnut oil
$\frac{1}{2}$ medium onion, peeled and finely chopped
$2\frac{1}{2}$ teacups hot chicken stock or water
$\frac{1}{2}$ level teaspoon salt
Freshly milled black pepper

Begin by melting the butter and oil in a thick-based saucepan and gently cooking the onion in it for about 5 minutes. Then add the rice and stir it around with a wooden spoon so that it gets a nice coating of butter. Now pour in the hot chicken stock and add seasoning. Stir just once, and when it reaches boiling point put a lid on and simmer gently for 20–25 minutes, or until all the liquid is absorbed and the rice is tender. Empty the rice into a serving dish and fluff the grains with a fork to separate them.

Onion Rice with Herbs This can be cooked as above, adding $\frac{1}{2}$ teaspoon of dried mixed herbs or 1 teaspoon of chopped fresh herbs.

Spiced Pilau Rice Again, cook as above, adding with the rice 2 whole cloves, a $1\frac{1}{2}$-inch (4-cm) piece of cinnamon stick and 1 teaspoon of powdered turmeric.

With all the above methods, if you use brown rice you'll need 40 minutes' cooking time and to use slightly less liquid, as in the following recipe.

Brown Rice Salad

(Serves 4)

1 teacup long-grain brown rice
1¾ teacups boiling water
3 or 4 tablespoons vinaigrette dressing (see page 143)
3 spring onions, very finely chopped
2 inches (5 cm) cucumber, finely chopped
2 large tomatoes, skinned and finely chopped
½ red or green pepper, de-seeded and finely chopped
1 red dessert apple, chopped but not peeled
1 oz (25 g) currants
1 oz (25 g) walnuts, finely chopped
Salt and freshly milled black pepper

Place the rice and some salt in a saucepan, pour the boiling water over and bring it back to the boil; then stir once, put a lid on and simmer very gently for 40 minutes or so until all the liquid has been absorbed. Now empty the rice into a salad bowl, fluff it up with a fork and pour the dressing over while it's still hot. Allow it to cool and then mix in all the other ingredients, adding a little more dressing it if needs it and tasting to check the seasoning. Keep in a cool place until needed.

Brown Rice with Vegetables (Serves 2)

Serve this with some good cheese and crusty bread to follow and I promise you won't miss the meat.

1 teacup long-grain brown rice
2 tablespoons butter
2 tablespoons oil
1 large green pepper, de-seeded and chopped
1 medium onion, peeled and roughly chopped
2 sticks celery, chopped
3 oz (75 g) mushrooms, sliced
2 teacups boiling stock (or water)
$\frac{1}{2}$ teaspoon dried thyme
Salt and freshly milled black pepper
3 tablespoons chopped parsley
6 spring onions, finely chopped (including green parts)

First heat the butter and oil in a large, solid saucepan, then add the prepared pepper, onion and celery to the pan and cook them over a *fairly* low heat until they're softened and slightly golden. Now put the rice in a sieve and rinse well with cold water. Drain it, shaking any excess water out, and add it to the saucepan, with the sliced mushrooms, stirring well. Cook for a minute or two before pouring in the stock. Add the thyme, season with salt and pepper, and bring to simmering point; then cover and cook very gently for about 35–40 minutes, or until the rice is just tender. As soon as the rice seems to be *almost* cooked, remove the lid from the pan and continue to cook until the rice is tender and free from any liquid. Then sprinkle in the parsley and the chopped spring onions. Taste and season with more salt and pepper if necessary.

Buttered Noodles with Meat Balls (Serves 4)

Serve these delicious little meat balls with ribbon noodles or spaghetti.

1 lb (450 g) ribbon noodles (or spaghetti)
Salt
A little oil
Butter

For the meat balls:
A $\frac{1}{2}$ inch (1 cm) thick slice of white bread with the crusts
  removed
3 or 4 tablespoons milk
$\frac{1}{2}$ lb (225 g) minced beef
$\frac{1}{2}$ lb (225 g) minced pork
1 small onion, peeled and finely chopped
2 tablespoons chopped parsley
$\frac{1}{4}$ teaspoon dried thyme
$\frac{1}{4}$ teaspoon freshly grated nutmeg
1 teaspoon salt
Freshly milled black pepper
1 egg, beaten
Seasoned plain flour
Oil for frying

For the sauce:
A 14 oz (400 g) tin Italian tomatoes
1 small onion, peeled and finely chopped
1 clove garlic, crushed
1 tablespoon oil
1 teaspoon dried basil
Salt and freshly milled black pepper

To make the sauce, soften the onion and garlic in the oil in a pan, then add the tomatoes, basil and seasoning and simmer without a lid for about 20 minutes. While it cooks, soak the bread in the milk for a few minutes, then squeeze out the milk and shred the bread into a large bowl. Mix the bread, minced meats, chopped onion, herbs and spices together with the beaten egg; form the mixture into meat balls a bit larger in size than a walnut—you'll find the mixture makes about 16. Roll the balls in seasoned flour, then heat some oil in a large frying pan and fry the meat balls in the hot fat until they are browned and cooked through (about 8–10 minutes). Boil the ribbon noodles (or spaghetti) in salted water with a few drops of oil added for 12 minutes. Then drain the meat balls well and keep them warm. Drain the ribbon noodles, toss them in butter, and serve them with the meat balls and the sauce.

Spaghetti Bolognese (Serves 4)

For the ragu Bolognese:
3 oz (75 g) chicken livers, chopped small
6 oz (175 g) lean minced beef
2 rashers streaky bacon (unsmoked), finely chopped
1 teaspoon dried basil
1 small onion, peeled and very finely chopped
An 8 oz (225 g) tin Italian tomatoes
1 fat clove garlic, crushed
4 tablespoons red wine
2 heaped tablespoons tomato purée
1½ tablespoons olive oil

And then:
1 lb (450 g) spaghetti
1 oz (25 g) butter
Some Parmesan cheese, grated
Salt and freshly milled black pepper

Begin by making the ragu: heat the olive oil in a thick-based saucepan and in it gently soften the onion, chopped bacon and garlic for 5 minutes. Turning the heat up, add the chicken livers together with the beef to brown (keeping everything on the move with a wooden spoon). When the meat has browned, add the contents of the tin of tomatoes along with the basil, red wine and tomato purée, and some seasoning, cover the saucepan and simmer gently for 20 minutes. After that time take off the lid and continue simmering gently for a further

20–25 minutes, so that the sauce can get nicely concentrated. Towards the end of this cooking time, fill a large saucepan with water, bring to the boil, add some salt and then the spaghetti (if you also add about a teaspoon of olive oil to the water, this will help prevent the pasta sticking together). When the spaghetti has sunk down into the water, stir thoroughly, then cover and simmer very gently for 12 minutes. Strain the cooked spaghetti in a warmed colander, add a knob of butter and a few twists of freshly milled pepper, then transfer on to warmed plates. Pour the sauce over and serve with grated Parmesan sprinkled over.

Spaghetti with Tuna and Olives   (Serves 3)

1 lb (450 g) spaghetti
A 7½ oz (210 g) can tuna in oil
1 large onion, peeled and chopped
1 clove garlic, crushed
4 oz (110 g) button mushrooms, quartered
1 lb (450 g) ripe tomatoes, skinned and chopped
1 tablespoon tomato purée
1 teaspoon dried basil
2 oz (50 g) green stuffed olives, chopped
Salt and freshly milled black pepper
A little butter
Some grated Parmesan cheese

First drain the oil from the tin of tuna into a saucepan, heat it gently and fry the onion and garlic until softened. Then add the mushrooms to the pan and cook for a further 2 or 3 minutes. Now pour the tomatoes into the pan, add the tuna, tomato purée and basil, then cover and cook for a further 10–15 minutes, or until the mixture has reduced to a nice consistency. Next add the olives, taste, and season with salt and pepper. Cook the spaghetti for 10–12 minutes in plenty of salted water, drain and toss a little butter in. Then season well with salt and pepper, and serve the spaghetti topped with the sauce and have some freshly grated Parmesan to go with it.

Macaroni Carbonara   (Serves 2)

I find this recipe indispensable for a delicious spur-of-the-moment meal that can be conjured up from ingredients I nearly always have in the house.

½ lb (225 g) any supermarket macaroni
4 oz (110 g) streaky bacon, chopped
2 large eggs
2 tablespoons grated Parmesan cheese
Butter
A little oil
Salt and freshly milled black pepper

Before you cook the macaroni, have ready a large mixing bowl which should be heated in a medium oven (mark 4/350°F/180°C). Then place the macaroni in a saucepan of briskly boiling water to which salt and a few drops of oil have been added. Cook it without a lid, according to the instructions on the packet (about 12 minutes). While that's happening, melt a little oil in a frying pan and cook the bacon—not crisply, just until the fat starts to run. Also break the eggs into a bowl, season them with salt and pepper, add the Parmesan and beat with a fork. Now put two plates in the oven to warm, then drain the cooked macaroni in a colander, whip the hot bowl out of the oven and tip the macaroni into it. Quickly add the bacon, followed by the beaten eggs—and stir it all around speedily and deftly. Continue stirring and the eggs will soon cook and turn slightly granular from the heat of the bowl. Serve on to warmed plates with a knob of butter on each serving, and have some extra grated Parmesan cheese on the table to sprinkle over.

Spaghetti with Olives and Anchovies

(Serves 2)

8 oz (225 g) spaghetti
3 tablespoons oil
8 oz (225 g) fresh mushrooms, thinly sliced
2 onions, peeled and thinly sliced
2 cloves garlic, crushed
5 anchovy fillets, snipped in half
3 rashers lean bacon, rinded and roughly chopped
Salt
2 tablespoons chopped parsley
6 Spanish stuffed olives, sliced
2 tablespoons grated Parmesan cheese

First of all, heat the oil in a thick-based pan and start to cook the mushrooms, onion, garlic, anchovy fillets and bacon gently. Stir them all around from time to time. Boil the spaghetti in salted water with 1 teaspoon of extra oil in it for 10 minutes. Then add the parsley and olives to the other ingredients in the pan and heat them through. Now drain the spaghetti in a warmed colander, pile it on to a warmed serving dish and top with the savoury mixture, sprinkled finally with the grated Parmesan cheese.

Macaroni au Gratin
(Serves 3)

4 oz (110 g) any supermarket macaroni
1½ pints (850 ml) water
2 oz butter
1½ oz (40 g) plain flour
1 level teaspoon mustard powder
¾ pint (420 ml) milk
6 oz (175 g) cheese (Cheddar), grated
A little freshly grated nutmeg
1 medium onion, peeled and chopped
4 rashers streaky bacon, rinded and chopped
2 oz (50 g) mushrooms, sliced
1 tomato, cut into small pieces
A little extra butter
Salt and freshly milled black pepper

Bring the water to the boil in a large pan with 1 teaspoon salt, add the macaroni and boil without a lid, according to the instructions on the packet. Meanwhile melt 2 oz (50 g) of butter in a saucepan, add the flour and mustard, and make up a white sauce with the milk, cooking for about 6 minutes before adding 3 oz (75 g) of the grated cheese to melt gently into it, together with a seasoning of salt and pepper and a few gratings of nutmeg. Then in a little butter in a small frying pan, soften the onion, bacon and mushroom together for about 6 minutes. Now drain the macaroni in a colander, combine it with the sauce and the bacon, onion and mushroom, then place the whole mixture in a buttered 2-pint (1.2-litre) baking dish. Sprinkle the rest of the cheese on top, plus the pieces of tomato. Finish off by placing the dish under a hot grill until golden brown and bubbling.

Note: If you want to make this in advance, you can re-heat it in a high oven, mark 6/400°F/200°C, for about 15–20 minutes.

I do, for one. I could never be an out-and-out vegetarian, although I must admit the thought does cross my mind from time to time. But then all I have to do is conjure up a picture of a steaming steak and kidney pud bursting at the seams with fragrant juices or imagine the sound and smell of bacon and eggs sizzling, and I'm instantly cured.

On the other hand, I also think our national preoccupation with excessive meat-eating is to some extent the result of habit. Once the habit is broken one can live quite happily for days with little or no meat, and I very often do. True, a main meal that doesn't contain any meat (or pulses, which we'll come to later) needs a little more care, needs to be, if you like, a little more special. The scope, however, is enormous: there are literally hundreds of variations on the quiche—just think what a treat a soufflé is, and if you've never tried your hand at a pizza I insist you try it now.

As for faint-hearted wives who complain that their husbands only want meat—well, I've never been liberated or concerned with women's rights, but I do think that if you're going to go to the trouble of cooking for someone the least they can do is eat what you cook. So be firm: send him off to buy his own steak and chops *and* pay for them. If not, blame it all on this book.

Pizza Dough

8 oz (225g) plain flour
1 level teaspoon salt
¼ teaspoon sugar
1½ teaspoons dried yeast
1 medium egg, beaten
3–4 fl (75–110ml) oz water (hand-hot)
1 teaspoon oil

First pour 3 fl oz (75ml) of hand-hot water into a basin and whisk in the sugar, followed by the yeast; then leave this mixture on one side for about 10–15 minutes until it gets a nice frothy head on it. Meanwhile sift the flour and salt together in a mixing bowl. Then pour in the frothy yeast mixture and the beaten egg, and mix to a dough (you may need to add just a spot of extra warm water—it depends on the flour—but at the end you should have a soft, pliable dough that leaves the bowl clean). Then transfer the dough to a working surface and knead for about 10 minutes until it's silky smooth and fairly elastic.

Now replace the dough in the bowl and rub the surface all over with the oil. Then seal the top of the bowl with cling film—or cover with a clean cloth—and put the dough in a warmish place to rise for about an hour, or until it has doubled in size.

Once the dough has 'proved' (that is, doubled in size), knead it again for about 5 minutes, and then it's ready to use. (All this does in fact *sound* a lot more trouble than it actually is.)

There are many different fillings for pizzas, but here are two combinations that I particularly like. Of course, you can adapt them, if you feel like it, and make up your own variations.

Pizza with Cream Cheese, Olives and Anchovies

(Serves 2–4)

For the tomato sauce:
2 tablespoons oil
1 Spanish onion, peeled and chopped
2 cloves garlic, crushed
2 × 14 oz (400 g) tins Italian tomatoes
¾ teaspoon dried basil (or fresh if you have it)
1 large bayleaf
Salt and freshly milled black pepper

For the garnish:
Oil
4 oz (110 g) cream cheese, cut in small pieces
A 2 oz (50 g) can anchovy fillets, drained and chopped
1 dozen black olives, pitted and halved
1 teaspoon dried oregano
1 tablespoon grated Parmesan

Make the pizza dough as described on page 169.

To prepare the sauce, heat the oil and fry the onion until softened and golden; then stir in the remaining sauce ingredients and simmer gently (uncovered) for about an hour, or until the tomatoes have reduced to a jam-like consistency. Then take the pan off the heat, discard the bayleaf and leave the sauce to cool.

Now select a large dry baking sheet (don't oil it) and push the dough out with your hands to a rectangle roughly 10 × 11 inches (25.5 × 28 cm)—or a round if you prefer. If the dough is very springy, be determined with it. Now pinch up the edges all round to make a sort of border to contain the filling. Then brush the base of the dough with oil, cover with the tomato filling and spread it right up to the pinched edge. Next sprinkle the surface with the cheese, anchovies, halved olives, dried oregano and Parmesan, drizzle about a tablespoon of oil over the top and leave the pizza at room temperature for 10 or 15 minutes before baking. Meanwhile pre-heat the oven to mark

7/425°F/220°C. Then bake the pizza for 15–20 minutes. Check that the bread base is cooked through in the centre by lifting the pizza up with a fish slice and taking a look. And remember it's better to slightly over-cook than under-cook a pizza, and always serve it fresh straight from the oven if possible.

Pizza with Salami and Mushrooms (Serves 2–4)

A 8 oz (225 g) tin Italian tomatoes
1 tablespoon tomato purée
1 teaspoon dried basil
6 oz (175 g) salami or Italian pepperoni sausage
1 small pepper, de-seeded and finely chopped
1 tablespoon capers
2 oz (50 g) mushrooms, thinly sliced
2 tablespoons grated Parmesan
Oil
Salt and freshly milled black pepper

Pre-heat the oven to mark 7/425°F/220°C

Prepare the pizza dough as described on page 169. Then choose a large baking sheet again, and push the dough out to a rectangle as in the previous recipe. Pinch out a narrow border and brush the base with oil. Now either liquidise the contents of the tin of tomatoes or simply rub them through a sieve into a bowl. Then stir in the tomato purée and basil, taste, and season with salt and freshly milled pepper. Now pour the mixture on to the pizza base and spread it all over. Next skin and thinly slice the salami, and halve the slices. Then arrange them over the top of the pizza, sprinkle on the chopped pepper, capers, sliced mushrooms and grated Parmesan, and again trickle a little oil over the top. Leave the pizza on one side for about 10 minutes before baking in the oven for 15–20 minutes.

Cheese and Vegetable Wholewheat Flan

(Serves 4)

For this recipe (ideal for vegetarians) I use a 7-inch (18-cm) metal pie plate with a rim which is about 1½ inches (4 cm) deep.

For the pastry:
1½ oz (40 g) wholewheat flour
1½ oz (40 g) plain flour
1½ oz (40 g) butter
A pinch salt
Some water

For the filling:
2 oz (50 g) butter
1 carrot, scraped and thinly sliced
3 oz (75 g) swede, peeled and thinly sliced
3 oz (75 g) turnip, peeled and thinly sliced
1 stick celery, sliced
1 small onion, peeled and finely chopped
1 small leek, trimmed, washed and finely chopped
2 oz (50 g) Cheddar cheese, grated
2 large eggs
8 fl oz (225 ml) milk
1 dessertspoon finely chopped parsley
2 pinches cayenne pepper
Salt and freshly milled black pepper

Pre-heat the oven to mark 4/350°F/180°C

First make the pastry (see page 212) and roll it out to line the tin. Then prick the pastry base and pre-cook it on a baking sheet for 15 minutes. While that's happening, melt the butter in a frying pan and soften all the vegetables in it for 10–15 minutes. Now remove the flan tin from the oven and, using a draining spoon, transfer the vegetables from the pan to the pastry case, season well and sprinkle the grated cheese on top. Next beat the eggs together with the milk, pour the mixture over the vegetables, then sprinkle with parsley and a couple of pinches of cayenne. Return it to the oven (at the same temperature) and bake for about 40 minutes until golden and puffy.

I like this served with some nice nutty brown rice cooked with onion and herbs (see page 157).

Courgette Soufflé   (Serves 4)

This will make a very impressive lunchtime dish for 4 people.

4 oz (110 g) courgettes, thinly sliced
4 oz butter
2 tablespoons finely chopped parsley
2 teaspoons finely chopped chives
3 tablespoons plain flour
$\frac{1}{2}$ pint (275 ml) milk
5 egg yolks
2 oz (50 g) cheese, grated
1 oz (25 g) Parmesan, grated
6 egg whites
Salt and freshly milled black pepper
Freshly grated nutmeg
A little extra butter

Pre-heat the oven to mark 6/400°F/200°C

For this you'll need a 2½-pint (1.5-litre) soufflé dish, buttered quite generously. Start by cooking the courgettes gently in 2 oz (50 g) of the butter. Cook them until softened and beginning to colour slightly, then remove them from the heat, season them with salt and pepper, and leave them to cool. Now melt the remaining 2 oz (50 g) of butter in a saucepan, stir in the flour and cook for a minute or two before gradually adding the milk, stirring all the time. Bring the mixture up to a simmer, still stirring, and let it cook for about 2 or 3 minutes. Take the sauce off the heat now and cool it by sitting the base of the pan in some cold water. As soon as it's cool enough, gradually beat in the egg yolks, followed by the cheeses, parsley and chives. Season with salt, pepper and freshly grated nutmeg. Now beat up the egg whites to the stiff peak stage and carefully fold them into the cheese mixture, using a metal spoon. Next spoon half the soufflé mixture into the prepared dish, sprinkle in the courgette slices and pour the remaining soufflé mixture on top of them. Now place the soufflé dish in a roasting tin, pour a little boiling water in the tin (to a depth of 1 inch/2.5 cm) and transfer the whole lot to the oven. Lower the heat to mark 3/325°F/170°C, bake for 40 minutes and then increase the heat to mark 6/400°F/200°C for a further 10 minutes.

Spinach Cream Flan   (Serves 6 as a main course)

If you can't get fresh spinach for this, use 1 lb (450 g) of frozen, well thawed and drained.

A quantity shortcrust pastry (made with 6 oz/175 g plain flour
    and 3 oz/75 g fat—see page 212)

For the filling:
2 lb (900 g) fresh spinach
1 oz (25 g) butter
$\frac{1}{2}$ lb (225 g) cream cheese
3 eggs, beaten
$\frac{1}{4}$ pint (150 ml) milk
Freshly grated nutmeg
2 tablespoons grated Parmesan or any mild cheese
Salt and freshly milled black pepper
A squeeze of lemon juice

Pre-heat the oven to mark 4/350°F/180°C with a baking sheet in it

Start by making the pastry, and line a 10-inch (25.5-cm) flan tin with it. Prick the pastry base, place the flan tin on the pre-heated baking sheet and bake it for 15 minutes. Then take it out of the oven, leave it on one side to cool and increase the oven heat to mark 5/375°F/190°C. Now prepare the filling by washing the spinach and discarding any coarse stalks or damaged leaves. Wash the leaves thoroughly, drain and place them in a large heavy-based saucepan with the butter and some salt and freshly ground black pepper. (No need to add any water.) Cover the pan and cook the spinach for about 7 minutes, shaking the pan occasionally, until the spinach collapses down into the butter.

Then drain the spinach in a colander very thoroughly, pressing out any excess moisture, and chop it up with a sharp knife. Now place the cream cheese in a bowl and beat in the milk a little at a time, followed by the beaten eggs, Parmesan cheese and a seasoning of salt, pepper and a little grated nutmeg. Now stir the spinach into the cream mixture. Add a squeeze of lemon juice and, if necessary, a bit more seasoning. Then pour the mixture into the flan case and place the flan back on the heated baking sheet. Bake in the top half of the oven for about 40 minutes, or until the filling is nice and puffy and golden on the top.

Soured Cream and Onion Tart

(Serves 4 as a main course)

A quantity shortcrust pastry (made with 6 oz/175 g plain flour and 3 oz/75 g fat—see page 212)

For the filling:
2 oz (50 g) butter
2 lb (900 g) onions, peeled and very thinly sliced
1 clove garlic, crushed
$\frac{1}{4}$ teaspoon dried sage
A 5 fl oz (150 ml) carton soured cream
2–3 tablespoons single cream (or top of the milk)
1 large egg
Salt and freshly milled black pepper

Pre-heat the oven to mark 4/350°F/180°C

First make the pastry as described on page 212, line a 10-inch (25.5-cm) flan tin with it, prick the base and bake it blind in the oven for 15 minutes. Then remove it from the oven and turn the heat up to mark 5/375°F/190°C and place a baking sheet in the oven.

Gently heat the butter in a large saucepan, and put the sliced onions, garlic and sage in the pan. Cover and cook over a low heat for about 15 minutes, shaking the pan occasionally. Then take the lid off and continue to cook (still shaking from time to time) for a further 15–20 minutes, or until the onions form a soft golden mass. Then remove from the heat. Now beat together the creams and egg, and stir this into the onions. Taste and season with salt and pepper. Spread the mixture in the pastry case. Then place the flan on the heated baking sheet in the top half of the oven and bake for about 40 minutes, or until the surface of the tart is lightly browned.

Leek, Carrot and Potato Pie (Serves 3)

This is a complete supper dish made from root vegetables— just the thing if you don't want a heavy meal.

1 lb (450 g) potatoes, peeled and left whole
$\frac{1}{2}$ lb (225 g) carrots, scraped and left whole
Butter
1 lb (450 g) leeks, halved lengthways and cut into $\frac{1}{4}$-inch (5-mm) thick slices
1 small onion, peeled and chopped
$\frac{1}{2}$ pint (275 ml) white sauce (made with $1\frac{1}{2}$ oz/40 g butter, $\frac{3}{4}$ oz/ 20 g plain flour, $\frac{1}{4}$ pint (150 ml) each of milk and vegetable stock, a pinch ground mace)
Salt and freshly milled black pepper

For the topping:
3 oz (75 g) Cheddar cheese, grated
1 tablespoon fresh white breadcrumbs
2 pinches cayenne pepper

Pre-heat the oven to mark 4/350°F/180°C

Bring a saucepan of salted water up to boiling point, then put in the whole potatoes and carrots; bring them to the boil, cover and cook for about 15 minutes. Then drain them, reserving the water. Now return the pan you cooked them in to the heat and melt 2 oz (50 g) of butter in it. Add the washed, drained leeks and the chopped onion, and cook them gently for about 6 or 7 minutes, or until softened. Now slice the potatoes and carrots thinly and arrange them in layers in a well-buttered baking dish. Then make up the sauce and pour it over the vegetables, scatter the cheese and breadcrumbs and a couple of pinches of cayenne on the top, dot the surface with small flecks of butter and bake for about 1 hour.

Curried Eggs with Cauliflower (Serves 3)

If you've got a few spices handy, this dish can be made fairly quickly with just a few eggs and a cauliflower, and it tastes quite delicious.

6 eggs
1 large cauliflower
1 tablespoon plain flour
1 oz (25 g) butter
1 tablespoon oil
1 onion, peeled and finely chopped
2 teaspoons ground coriander
1 teaspoon turmeric
1 clove garlic, crushed
$\frac{1}{4}$–$\frac{1}{2}$ teaspoon chilli powder (how much depends on you)
$\frac{1}{2}$ pint (275 ml) stock (from the cauliflower water)
2–3 teaspoons mango chutney
A squeeze of lemon juice
2 tablespoons natural yoghurt
Salt

Begin by dividing the cauliflower into small florets. Have ready some boiling, salted water and cook them in it for about 5 minutes. Then drain them and reserve the water. Next heat the butter and oil in a large cooking pot and gently fry the onion until soft; stir in the garlic, spices and flour, and cook for a minute or two before gradually stirring in $\frac{1}{2}$ pint (275 ml) of the cauliflower water. Now bring up to the boil, cover and simmer very gently for 10 minutes. Then stir in the chutney, lemon juice, yoghurt and cauliflower, and cook for a further 5 minutes, tasting to check the seasoning. At some time while all this is happening, carefully lower the eggs into a pan of gently simmering water, simmer for 7 minutes, then cool them under running water. Peel off the shells, halve the eggs and arrange them on a warmed serving dish. Pour the sauce and cauliflower over the top. Serve with rice and mango chutney.

Pancakes with Spinach and Cheese (Serves 2 or 3)

For a complete meal all this needs is a lot of crusty bread and butter and some fresh fruit to follow.

6 thin pancakes (see page 220)
1½ lb (700 g) fresh spinach
3 tablespoons butter
4–5 tablespoons double cream
¾ pint (420 ml) cheese sauce (made with 2 oz/50 g butter, 1½ oz/ 40 g plain flour, ¾ pint/420 ml milk and 3 oz/75 g grated cheese)
1 oz (25 g) Parmesan, grated
Freshly grated nutmeg
Salt and freshly milled black pepper
A little extra butter

Pre-heat the oven to mark 6/400°F/200°C

First prepare the spinach by washing it in several changes of water. Discard any damaged leaves and pick out any thick stalks. Press the leaves firmly into a large saucepan and sprinkle with about a teaspoon of salt. Don't add any water, just cover the pan and cook over a fairly high heat for about 7 or 8 minutes. While it cooks, remove the lid once or twice and turn the spinach around a bit with a wooden spoon. Then drain the spinach in a colander, pressing out as much excess liquid as possible. Now chop the spinach, melt 3 tablespoons of the butter in a frying pan and add the chopped spinach to the pan, followed by the cream. Stir (a wooden fork is good here to break up the spinach) and cook until there is no excess cream and you have a nice moist mixture to fill the pancakes. Taste and season with salt and freshly milled pepper, and a good grating of whole nutmeg. Now arrange an equal quantity of the spinach mixture on each pancake and roll them up; then place them in a well-buttered gratin dish and pour over the prepared sauce. Finally sprinkle the surface with the grated cheese and bake near the top of the oven for 25 minutes, until it's nicely browned and bubbling.

Baked Marrow with Sage and Cheese (Serves 4)

This is an excellent meatless supper dish, especially when marrows are very cheap around the latter half of August.

A 3¼-lb (1.4 kg) marrow
4 oz (110 g) Wensleydale cheese, grated
¾ teaspoon dried sage
1 medium onion, peeled and thinly sliced
3 tablespoons fresh white breadcrumbs
Salt and freshly milled black pepper

Pre-heat the oven to mark 2/300°F/150°C

Trim off both ends of the marrow and peel it, using a potato peeler if you've got one; then halve the marrow lengthways and scoop out and discard all the fibre and seeds. Now cut it into ¼-inch (5 mm) thick slices and then halve the slices. Put a third of the marrow in a layer in the base of a 4-pint (2.25 litre) casserole. Sprinkle with a third of the grated cheese, ¼ teaspoon of sage, half the sliced onion and a little salt and pepper. Repeat this layering once more, then finish off with a layer of marrow and some seasoning. Next mix the remaining cheese with the breadcrumbs and sprinkle all over the top. Cover loosely with a sheet of foil and bake for 1 hour. Then uncover and bake for a further hour, or until the vegetables are tender when tested with a skewer. Serve hot—or it's even nicer served cold if the weather's very hot.

QUICKENING PULSES

There was a startling report by the Consumers' Association in 1976 which stated that anyone in this country could survive (foodwise) on £2 per week! What's more they told us how, and one of the top-rated foods for protein and value were the various pulses (or legumes as they're sometimes called): lentils, dried peas, beans, etc.

It wasn't so long ago that these raw materials were overlooked by all except vegetarians. Nowadays, not only are they highly regarded as important sources of protein but also the path-finders of commercialism have begun to use these vegetable proteins to make imitation meat. Never mind if meat is short, they say, we'll just *pretend* we've got it. So Britain was presented with her first samples of TVP (textured vegetable protein), and the Press with a host of funny 'can-you-tell-the-difference' stories.

Nutritionists (often indirectly on the payrolls of the companies producing TVP) said we were all going to *have* to eat it for future survival. Happily, it hasn't yet caught on (not that producers are deterred—it took 100 years for margarine to be universally accepted). In spite of all the nice people who have tried hard to convince me, the facts as I see them are these:

(a) If we can't have meat in the future, then let's not pretend we can—let's evolve in a more realistic direction.

(b) Vegetable proteins (as in this chapter) can be cooked and eaten as they are without the expense of refining and disguising them.

(c) The promoters of TVP point out that it's not meant to be eaten on its own, it's meant to extend meat. As a cook I'm bound to say there are far pleasanter ways of eking out meat if it's simply for bulk; ordinary vegetables, onion, carrot, celery, turnip, swede, all add flavours of their own. And if it's to increase protein, then why not add our pulses as they are, with their own flavour and texture? It might not be so convenient in the school canteen, but at least our children would be pointed in the right direction for the future instead of being deceived by pretend meat.

And now I'm off my soap-box, one positive aspect of the situation is that farmers are at last experimenting with lentil production in this country, and I'm told that soya production may well yield over a ton an acre within a few years. I hope they succeed.

Chilladas

(Serves 4)

These little lentil rissoles are, in my opinion, even better than those made with meat, and they're delicious served with the Tomato and Chilli Sauce on page 145.

8 oz (225 g) green or brown whole lentils
$\frac{3}{4}$ pint (420 ml) hot water
2 oz (50 g) butter or vegetable margarine
1 medium onion, peeled and finely chopped
1 clove garlic, crushed
1 medium carrot, scraped and finely chopped
1 small green pepper, de-seeded and chopped small
$\frac{1}{2}$ teaspoon cayenne pepper
$\frac{1}{4}$ teaspoon powdered mace
$\frac{1}{2}$ teaspoon mixed herbs
2 teaspoons tomato purée
Salt and freshly milled black pepper

Then:
1 egg, beaten
Dry fine breadcrumbs
Enough groundnut oil for shallow-frying

Wash and pick over the lentils, then place them in a saucepan with the hot water and some salt. When they come to the boil, cover and simmer very gently for about an hour, or until all the liquid has been absorbed and the lentils are mushy. Towards the end of their cooking time, heat the butter or magarine in a frying pan and soften the onion, garlic and carrot in it for 5 minutes; then add the chopped pepper and cook for a further 5 or 10 minutes. Next tip the cooked lentils into a bowl and mash them to a pulp with a fork (not too uniformly smooth). Now mix in the softened vegetables, cayenne, mace, herbs and tomato purée, then divide the mixture and shape into 12 small rounds. All this can be done in advance. To cook them, dip them first in beaten egg, then in breadcrumbs. Shallow-fry them in about $\frac{1}{4}$ inch (5 mm) of groundnut oil till golden on both sides, then drain on kitchen paper and serve with the sauce.

Chick Pea Salad

(Serves 4–6)

$\frac{1}{2}$ lb (225 g) chick peas (soaked overnight)
$\frac{1}{2}$ (225 g) haricots verts (green string beans)
$\frac{1}{4}$ pint (150 ml) garlic-flavoured mayonnaise
A 2 oz (50 g) tin anchovy fillets, drained and finely chopped
6 spring onions, finely chopped
2 tablespoons capers, chopped
2 tablespoons finely chopped parsley
A dozen pitted black olives, halved
Lemon juice to taste
A few crisp lettuce leaves
Salt and freshly milled black pepper

Bring the chick peas to the boil and simmer until tender (about 30–45 minutes). Don't salt the water, though, or the chick peas will not soften. The topped and tailed haricots will need 3 or 4 minutes in boiling salted water, then drain them with cold water and cut each bean in half. Combine the mayonnaise, anchovy fillets, spring onions, capers, chopped parsley, and add salt and pepper. Then fold the drained chick peas and green beans into the mayonnaise mixture together with the black olives. Taste and add a little lemon juice and more seasoning if necessary. Serve on a bed of crisp lettuce leaves.

Boston Baked Beans

(Serves 4)

This is how Baked Beans should be, the real American sort not a bit like the ones that come in tins.

1 lb (450 g) dried white haricot beans
3 pints (1.7 litres) water
1 onion, peeled and sliced
2 cloves garlic, crushed
1 bayleaf
1 teaspoon English mustard powder
2 tablespoons black treacle
2 tablespoons dark brown sugar
2 tablespoons tomato purée
¾ lb (350 g) streaky belly of pork, in one piece
Salt and freshly milled black pepper

Measure the water into a large saucepan, add the beans, bring to the boil and boil gently for about 2–3 minutes; then remove the pan from the heat and leave on one side for about 1 hour, or until the water has cooled. Now return the beans to the heat and simmer uncovered until the bean skins burst when you lift them out of the water (which will take around 45 minutes). Drain the beans next, reserving the liquor, then measure the liquor and make it up to 1 pint (570 ml) with water if necessary. Transfer the beans to a casserole and pre-heat the oven to mark ½/250°F/120°C.

At this stage, blend the mustard powder with a little of the measured bean liquor, followed by the black treacle, sugar, tomato purée and crushed garlic, and pour this mixture over the beans along with the measured pint of liquid, some seasoning, the sliced onion and a bayleaf. Now cut slashes across the pork (approximately ½ inch/1 cm apart) and bury the meat in the beans until only the rind is showing. Then cover the casserole closely and bake very slowly for about 6 hours. During the last hour of cooking, take the lid off the casserole to allow the rind on the pork to crisp a little. Also keep stirring the beans during this last hour and, if it shows signs of getting too dry, add just a spot more water. Serve very hot.

Dhal Curry

Dhal is simply the Indian word for lentils. The best kind to use for this are the red split lentils which most supermarkets stock.

8 oz (225 g) red lentils
1 teaspoon each ground ginger, ground cumin, turmeric and salt
2 potatoes, peeled and diced
2 tablespoons butter
1 large onion, sliced
1 small green pepper, de-seeded and chopped
1 level teaspoon Madras curry powder (if you like your curries hotter, you can add more)
1 clove garlic, crushed
1 extra teaspoon ground ginger
4 tomatoes, peeled and chopped

In a saucepan containing $1\frac{1}{2}$ pints (850 ml) of water add the ginger, cumin, turmeric and salt, then bring it all to the boil. Stir in the lentils, let it come back to a gentle simmer and cook for 5 minutes. After that add the diced potato and continue cooking until the lentils have turned mushy (making sure the mixture doesn't stick to the bottom of the pan by giving it a stir now and again). While that's cooking, heat up the butter in another pan and fry the onion and pepper in it (over a fairly high heat) until the onion has browned—then lower the heat and stir in the Madras curry powder, the garlic, extra ground ginger and chopped tomatoes. Cook for a minute before adding the lentil mixture, then taste, season with more salt and cook gently for a further 5–10 minutes (stirring from time to time). Serve this with rice and yoghurt.

Spiced Chick Pea Cutlets (Serves 3)

Chick peas, sometimes called garbanzos, need a long soaking, so try to think ahead.

8 oz (225 g) chick peas (soaked overnight in plenty of cold water)
2 tablespoons oil
1 onion, peeled and finely chopped
1 small green pepper, de-seeded and finely chopped
1 clove garlic, crushed
2 teaspoons tomato purée
2 tablespoons natural yoghurt
$\frac{1}{2}$ teaspoon Madras curry powder
$\frac{1}{2}$ teaspoon cayenne pepper
Dry white breadcrumbs (for coating)
Oil for shallow-frying
Salt and freshly milled black pepper

First tip the soaked chick peas, and their water, into a saucepan. Bring them up to the boil, cover and simmer for about 30 minutes, or until they're absolutely tender. Then drain well, and mash them to a pulp. Now put the 2 tablespoons of oil in a saucepan and gently fry the onion and green pepper until softened; then beat them into the mashed chick peas together with all the remaining ingredients (except, of course, the breadcrumbs and frying oil). Do a bit of tasting at this stage, and season with some salt and pepper. As soon as it's cool enough to handle, form the mixture into 6 patties and coat each one with breadcrumbs. Put about 2 tablespoons of oil in a frying pan and fry the patties to a golden brown colour. Serve them hot garnished with slices of raw Spanish onion and some natural yoghurt as a sauce.

White Bean and Salami Salad (Serves 4)

This is a delicious salad to serve at lunchtime at any time of the year but especially in the summer. Make sure you have plenty of crusty bread to go with it to mop up the juices.

1 lb (450 g) dried large haricot beans
1 onion, peeled and stuck with 6 cloves
A few parsley stalks
1 bayleaf
1 clove garlic, crushed
½ teaspoon dried thyme or a sprig of fresh

For the dressing:
1 teaspoon salt
2 tablespoons wine vinegar
2 tablespoons dry cider
1 teaspoon mustard powder
1 clove garlic, crushed
¼ pint (150 ml) oil—olive or groundnut
Freshly milled black pepper

Then:
1 medium onion, peeled and thinly sliced
4 oz (110 g) salami, chopped small
1 tablespoon chopped fresh parsley

First put the dried beans in a sieve and wash them under cold running water. Then place them in a saucepan, add enough cold water to come up about 2 inches (5 cm) above the beans and bring to the boil. As soon as the water boils, switch off the heat and leave the beans to soak for about an hour. Then add the onion stuck with cloves, the parsley, bayleaf, garlic and thyme. Bring the beans back to the boil and simmer very gently without a lid for 1–1½ hours, or until the beans are tender. The length of cooking time really depends on the age of the beans. While the beans are cooking you can make the dressing by dissolving the salt in the wine vinegar for about half an hour and then adding all the other ingredients. To blend them, shake them in a screw-topped jar, then taste and add more pepper and salt if you think it needs it because this dressing needs to be very well seasoned. When the beans are cooked, drain them, and whilst they are still warm combine them with the dressing in a large mixing bowl. Mix them gently to avoid the beans breaking, then add the onion, salami and parsley, and leave for at least an hour before serving.

Lentil, Bean and Anchovy Salad (Serves 4)

This makes a very inexpensive lunch dish for 4 people along with some crusty bread to mop up the juices.

8 oz (225 g) white haricot beans
8 oz (225 g) whole lentils (brown)
Salt and freshly milled black pepper

For the dressing:
8 tablespoons oil
1 tablespoon wine vinegar
1 tablespoon lemon juice
1 small onion, peeled and finely chopped
1 heaped teaspoon made mustard
1 clove garlic, crushed
4 tablespoons finely chopped fresh parsley

To garnish:
A 2 oz (50 g) can anchovy fillets
A few crisp lettuce leaves
2 hardboiled eggs, chopped
1 oz (25 g) small black olives

In advance you'll need to put the beans in a saucepan with plenty of cold water to cover, then bring to the boil, boil for 2–3 minutes and remove them from the heat. Leave them for about an hour to soak, then boil them again until *just* soft, probably another hour. There's no need to soak the lentils: just pick over them, wash them and boil them in plenty of water until again *just* soft (about 25 minutes). Meanwhile make up the dressing by mixing everything together in a bowl and adding the oil from the tin of anchovies as well. (Chop the anchovies and keep them on one side.) As soon as the beans and lentils are cooked, drain them, and while they're still warm pour on the dressing, toss them around in it and leave to cool. Then taste and season the mixture well with salt and freshly milled pepper. To serve, place some of the bean-and-lentil mixture on to crisp lettuce leaves divided between 4 plates and garnish with the chopped hardboiled eggs, chopped anchovies and olives.

Curried Egg and Lentil Patties   (Serves 3)

$\frac{1}{4}$ lb (110 g) green or brown whole lentils
3 medium eggs, hardboiled and chopped
1 largish onion, peeled and finely chopped
1 clove garlic, crushed
2 oz (50 g) butter or margarine
1 tablespoon chopped fresh parsley
$\frac{1}{8}-\frac{1}{4}$ teaspoon chilli powder
$\frac{1}{4}$ teaspoon ground cumin
$\frac{1}{4}$ teaspoon ground coriander
$\frac{1}{4}$ teaspoon ground ginger
$\frac{1}{4}$ teaspoon turmeric
Salt and freshly milled black pepper
1 egg, beaten
Wholemeal flour
Groundnut oil for frying

Cook the lentils till mushy, as in the previous recipe, then soften the onion and garlic in the butter, add them to the lentils with the chopped eggs, spices, parsley, salt and pepper, and mix thoroughly. When cool, shape the mixture into 9 little patties. Dip them first in beaten egg, then in wholemeal flour and shallow-fry them till golden on both sides. Drain on kitchen paper and serve on a bed of spiced pilau rice (see page 157), garnished with slices of raw onion, and eat with mango chutney and a dollop of natural yoghurt.

Lentil and Split Pea Loaf (Serves 4)

This is nice served with tomato sauce or some yoghurt and is equally good eaten cold with salad or taken on a picnic in the summer.

6 oz (175 g) green or brown lentils
4 oz (110 g) split peas (yellow or green), picked over and rinsed
1 pint (570 ml) vegetable stock or water
$\frac{1}{4}$ teaspoon thyme
$\frac{1}{4}$ teaspoon marjoram
1 oz (25 g) butter
1 medium onion, peeled and chopped
$\frac{1}{2}$ green pepper, de-seeded and chopped
2 carrots, scraped and chopped
2 sticks celery, chopped
1 fat clove garlic, crushed
1 egg, beaten
2 tablespoons chopped parsley
Salt and freshly milled black pepper

Pre-heat the oven to mark 5/375°F/190°C

First bring the stock or water up to boiling point, then stir in the split peas and simmer (with a lid on) for about 5 minutes. Next add the lentils, thyme and marjoram and simmer, covered, for a further 25–30 minutes, or until all the liquid has been absorbed and the lentils and peas are soft; then remove the pan from the heat. Now, in another pan, heat the butter and fry all the prepared vegetables and garlic until golden—about 10 minutes. Then stir the mixture into the lentils with the beaten egg and parsley. Taste and season with salt and freshly milled pepper. Spoon the mixture into a well-greased 1-lb (450-g) loaf tin, cover with foil and bake for 40 minutes. When it's cooked, slip a knife around the inside edge and turn out on to a warmed serving plate.

Haricot and Lentil Chilli (Serves 4)

Whether you're a vegetarian or not, some meals without meat will eventually become a necessity—but that does not mean they can't be just as good, as this proves.

4 oz (110 g) haricot beans
4 oz (110 g) whole brown or green lentils
2 oz (50 g) pearl barley
2 oz (50 g) butter
1 large onion, peeled and chopped
2 cloves garlic, crushed
3 carrots, scraped and thinly sliced
4 sticks celery, sliced across thinly
A 14-oz (400-g) tin Italian tomatoes
1 tablespoon tomato purée
$\frac{1}{4}$–$\frac{1}{2}$ teaspoon chilli powder
1 bayleaf
1 green pepper, de-seeded and chopped
Salt and freshly milled black pepper

First of all put the haricot beans in a small saucepan with
plenty of cold water to cover, then bring them to the boil and
boil gently for 2 or 3 minutes. Remove them from the heat,
cover and leave on one side to soak for about an hour. After
that bring them to the boil again, cover and simmer for 30
minutes; then strain the beans, reserving all their liquor. While
all this is happening, you can very carefully pick over the
lentils, then put them in a sieve with the pearl barley and rinse
thoroughly under the cold water tap. Transfer them to a bowl,
pour some boiling water over them to cover and leave them to
soak for half an hour; then drain them, this time discarding the
water. Now heat the butter until frothy in a casserole and
gently soften the onion, garlic, carrot and celery (but don't
brown them). Then add the tomatoes and purée, and stir in
the drained lentils and barley, and the drained beans and their
reserved cooking liquor (made up to $\frac{1}{2}$ pint/275 ml with fresh
water). Now sprinkle in the chilli powder, add the bayleaf,
bring to simmering point, cover and continue to simmer for
half an hour. Then add the chopped pepper and continue to
simmer for a further 30 minutes, or until everything is just
tender. Taste and season with salt and pepper. Add a little
more water if you feel it's needed. Re-heat and serve with
some nutty brown rice cooked with onion.

Lentil and Vegetable Curry (Serves 6)

½ lb (225 g) runner beans, stringed and sliced
½ lb (225 g) potatoes, peeled and diced into ½-inch (1-cm)
  pieces
2 medium carrots, scraped and sliced
½ lb (225 g) cauliflower, separated into small florets
4 tablespoons oil
1 large onion, peeled and chopped
2 teaspoons turmeric
½ teaspoon ground coriander
2 teaspoons cumin seeds
2 teaspoons finely chopped fresh ginger (or 1 teaspoon
  ground)
1 fat clove garlic, crushed
12 oz (350 g) brown lentils (picked over and rinsed)
½ pint (275 ml) natural yoghurt
1 rounded tablespoon tomato purée
Salt
½–¾ teaspoon cayenne pepper

Blanch the beans, potatoes, carrots and cauliflower by placing them in a pan containing 1¾ pints (1 litre) of boiling salted water. Cover and cook gently for 6 minutes; then drain, reserving the water. Now heat the oil in a pan and fry the onion until softened. Then stir in the turmeric, coriander, cumin seeds, ginger and garlic, followed by the lentils, and stir until everything is thoroughly combined before pouring in the reserved vegetable water. Now bring to the boil, cover and cook gently for 40 minutes, or until the lentils are just tender. Next add the blanched vegetables to the lentil mixture along with the yoghurt, tomato purée and just ½ teaspoon of cayenne pepper. Stir well, and try to push all the vegetables below the surface of the liquid. Now bring to simmering point, cover and cook for a further 20 minutes, or until everything is tender. Taste and add a further ¼ teaspoon of cayenne, if you prefer a hotter flavour, and season with salt. Serve with rice.

BACK TO BAKING

As I see it, there are two important reasons for home baking.
One is that as often as not 50 per cent of the shop price can be

saved; the other is that it's almost always bound to taste better. As ever, time is the enemy, but quite honestly how much time does it really take to make a few biscuits, a cake and perhaps a few scones? Grandma's 'baking-day' principle still holds good—perhaps more so now that fuel prices have risen. Once the oven is on, it's best to make full use of it and pop in a batch of baking (provided you have a few airtight tins to keep your biscuits, cakes, etc. in).

I find home baking particularly self-satisfying and a great incentive to revive that neglected meal, the British Tea, especially at weekends. As for baking bread, if you've never made bread in your life I guarantee you'll find it a whole lot easier than it sounds (not to say cheaper, and so delicious that everyone will eat far too much of it and not be able to manage anything else!).

Strawberry Jam Sponge

I've always found the classic Victoria Sponge very dull and, frankly, not worth the trouble. Then along came soft margarine, and now it takes 2 minutes to whip up a sponge that's light, moist and keeps perfectly fresh in an airtight tin.

4 oz (110 g) self-raising flour
1 level teaspoon baking powder
4 oz (110 g) soft margarine at room temperature
4 oz (110 g) caster sugar
2 large eggs
2–3 drops vanilla essence

Pre-heat the oven to mark 3/325°F/170°C

For this you will need two 7-inch (18-cm) sponge tins, lightly buttered and their bases lined with greaseproof paper (these tins should be no less than $1\frac{1}{2}$ inches/4-cm deep. The size of the tins in cake making is absolutely vital—and no other sizes will do.

Combine all the ingredients in a mixing bowl and whisk with an electric hand-whisk for about 2 minutes, or until everything is thoroughly mixed. Now divide the mixture between the two prepared tins, level off and bake on the centre shelf of the oven for about 30 minutes. When cooked, leave them in the tins for only about 30 seconds before turning them out on to a wire cooling tray. When cool, sandwich together with strawberry jam, dust the top with sifted icing sugar and store in an airtight tin.

Sticky Tea Bread

This is unbelievably simple to make—it's dark and sticky and gets much better with a few days' keeping.

$\frac{1}{4}$ pint (150 ml) water
5 oz (150 g) caster sugar
4 oz (110 g) sultanas
$\frac{1}{4}$ lb (110 g) butter
1 teaspoon bicarbonate of soda
1 egg, beaten
1 teaspoon baking powder
6 oz (175 g) plain flour

Pre-heat the oven to mark 4/350°F/180°C

First grease a 1-lb (450-g) loaf tin and line it with greaseproof paper, also greased. Then take a large thick-based saucepan and put into it the water, sugar, sultanas, butter and bicarbonate of soda. Place the pan on a medium heat, stir the ingredients together and bring them up to the boil. Then boil for 10 minutes exactly—but don't go away, watch it like a hawk, because if the temperature isn't controlled it might boil over. When the 10 minutes is up, remove the pan from the heat and allow the mixture to cool. Then add the beaten egg, and the baking powder and flour sifted. Give it a good mix, then place the mixture in the prepared tin and bake it for about $1\frac{1}{2}$ hours on the middle shelf.

Irish Soda Bread

This is a good, easy, standby recipe for days when you suddenly need extra bread and you have no yeast available. It isn't a 'keeping' loaf, though, and is best eaten fresh.

8 oz (225 g) wholemeal flour
8 oz (225 g) plain flour
1 level teaspoon salt
1 teaspoon bicarbonate of soda
1 teaspoon sugar
2 teaspoons cream of tartar
2 oz (50 g) butter
½ pint (275 ml) milk

Pre-heat the oven to mark 5/375°F/190°C

First take a large bowl and sift the flours, salt, bicarbonate of soda, sugar and cream of tartar into it; then rub in the butter, using your fingertips, until it is thoroughly blended. Now mix in the milk, first with a wooden spoon then with your hands, until you have a nice soft dough; then knead it for a minute or two in the bowl, sprinkling in a little more flour if it feels sticky. Transfer the dough on to a lightly floured board and shape it neatly into a round. Now, using the back of a knife, score the top of the dough quite deeply, making a cross, and leave it for 10 minutes. After that, place the loaf on a greased baking sheet and bake it for about 30–40 minutes, or until it sounds hollow when tapped underneath. Then wrap it in a clean teacloth to keep the steam in, allow it to cool and serve it as fresh as possible.

Sugarless Orange and Sultana Cake

This recipe was snipped out of the *Evening Standard* in 1940 by a reader and it was very popular during the 1974 sugar crisis.

3 oz (75 g) margarine or butter
¼ pint (150 ml) sweetened condensed milk
2 eggs, whisked until frothy
6 oz (175 g) self-raising flour
4 oz (110 g) sultanas
Grated rind of 1 orange
1 tablespoon orange juice
Melted lard or butter

Pre-heat the oven to mark 3/325°F/170°C

Line the base of a deep, round 7-inch (18-cm) cake tin with a circle of greaseproof paper and brush the tin and paper with melted fat. Now place the butter (or margarine) in a bowl and beat until softened and light. Then gradually beat in the condensed milk, followed by the beaten eggs, a little at a time. Now carefully fold in the sifted flour, sultana, orange rind and juice. Mix thoroughly and spoon the mixture into the prepared tin. Bake in the centre of the oven for 1 hour, or until the cake shows signs of shrinking away from the side of the tin and is nicely risen and browned. Then turn the cake out on to a wire rack and leave to cool.

Wheatmeal Shortbread

If you're hard up and need to give someone a present, this would be ideal packed in a pretty tin. It is, in fact, a variation on the usual Scotch shortbread, only using brown flour and sugar, and some rice flour to give an extra crisp bite to it.

5 oz (150 g) butter (room temperature)
6 oz (175 g) wheatmeal flour (85 per cent flour), or 4 oz (110 g) wholemeal and 2 oz (50 g) plain white
2 oz (50 g) ground rice
2 oz (50 g) caster sugar
$\frac{1}{4}$ teaspoon salt
A little extra caster sugar

Pre-heat the oven to mark 3/325°F/170°C

Begin by beating the butter in a bowl and gradually working in the flour, ground rice, sugar and salt (using your hands at the end to form the mixture into a stiff dough)—but don't work it too much or the butter will get oily. Then divide the dough in half, and roll out one piece to a 6-inch (15-cm) round. Now transfer the round to a greased baking sheet, pinching all round the edge to decorate. Then, using the back of a knife, mark the round into 8 wedges, and prick all over with a fork. Do the same with the remaining piece of dough, then sprinkle both rounds with a little caster sugar. Now bake just below the centre of the oven for 40–45 minutes, or until both short-breads are tinged brown and feel firm in the centre. Then remove them from the oven, sprinkle again with a little more caster sugar and leave till cooled a little before cutting each round into the marked wedges. Cool them on a wire rack and store in an airtight tin. If you prefer, you can roll the dough out to a $\frac{1}{2}$-inch (1-cm) thick round and cut the shortbread into wedges with a small fluted cutter.

Quick Wholemeal Bread

This recipe is one I have adapted from one given by Doris Grant in her excellent book on wholefoods, *Your Daily Food*. For it you will need a 2-lb (900-g) loaf tin (well greased and warmed slightly) or two 1-lb (450-g) loaf tins.

1 lb (450 g) stoneground wholewheat flour
1 teaspoon salt
12 fl oz (350 ml) hand-hot water (i.e. water that you can hold
  your finger in for a few moments without burning it)
1 teaspoon dark brown sugar
2 level teaspoons dried yeast

Pre-heat the oven to mark 6/400°F/200°C

Carefully measure the flour into a mixing bowl (slightly warm the flour first in cold weather), and add the salt. Now pour $\frac{1}{4}$ pint (150 ml) of the water into a jug, add the dark brown sugar, sprinkle in the dried yeast, then stir well. Then leave it on one side for 10–15 minutes until it displays a good frothy head. When it's ready, pour the yeast liquid into the flour (mixing with a wooden spoon), then add the rest of the water gradually to make a dough that is slightly moister than usual but will eventually leave the bowl clean. Place the dough in the slightly warmed loaf tin(s), even it out, cover with a clean cloth, then leave in a warm place for about 25 minutes—or until the dough has risen to within an inch (2.5 cm) of the top of the tin. Finally, dust the top with a little wholewheat flour and bake on a high shelf in the oven for 40–45 minutes, 30–35 minutes if using 1lb (450 g) tins. To test if it is cooked, take the bread out of the tin and tap the underneath—you should get a hollow sound. Then leave it to cool on a wire tray.

Note: If the dough takes longer to rise than expected, don't worry, just leave it until it *is* within an inch (2.5 cm) of the top of the tin.

Date, Prune and Walnut Loaf

This is a nice nutty wholemeal cake, delicious cut in thick slices and spread with butter.

3 oz (75 g) dried prunes, soaked overnight
Butter (room temperature)
6 oz (175 g) soft brown sugar
2 eggs, lightly beaten
4 oz (110 g) wholewheat flour
4 oz (110 g) plain flour
A pinch salt
1 level teaspoon baking powder
3 oz (75 g) pitted dates
4 oz (110 g) walnuts, roughly chopped
3 or 4 tablespoons milk

Pre-heat the oven to mark 4/350°F/180°C

First well butter a 5 × 9-inch (13 × 23-cm) loaf tin. Then after soaking the prunes, drain them thoroughly, take out the stones and chop the flesh into largish pieces. Now in a large mixing bowl cream 4 oz (110 g) of the butter and the sugar together till pale white and fluffy, then add the beaten eggs a little at a time, beating well after each addition. Next sift the flours, salt and baking powder and, using a metal spoon, fold them carefully into the creamed mixture. Now add the prunes, dates and walnuts, followed by the milk, and mix them in before transferring the mixture to the tin. Spread it out evenly, then bake for 1 hour, or until the loaf feels springy in the centre and a skewer inserted in the middle comes out clean. Let the cake cool for a minute or two in the tin, then turn it out on to a wire tray to cool and store in an airtight tin.

Old-fashioned Seed Cake

I think this is best kept in an airtight tin to mature for a couple of days.

4 oz (110g) butter
4 oz (110g) caster sugar
2 eggs, beaten
1 oz (25g) ground almonds
2 teaspoons caraway seeds
5 oz (150g) self-raising flour
2–3 tablespoons milk
12 sugar cubes, lightly crushed with a rolling pin
Little extra butter for greasing

Pre-heat the oven to mark 4/350°F/180°C

Start by buttering a 7-inch (18-cm) round cake tin and lining the base with a circle of greaseproof paper cut to fit; then butter the paper too. Cream the butter and caster sugar together until the mixture is pale and fluffy. Then beat in the eggs a little at a time, and lightly fold in the ground almonds, caraway seeds and flour, followed by enough milk to give the mixture a good dropping consistency. Now spoon the mixture into the prepared tin, level off the surface with the back of a tablespoon and sprinkle with the crushed sugar cubes. Bake the cake in the centre of the oven for about 1 hour, or until the cake feels springy in the centre and shows signs of shrinking away from the side of the tin. Cool on a wire rack.

Oat Crunch Biscuits

Making these delicious little biscuits at home will cost you half what you would pay in the shops. These ingredients are enough for 12 biscuits.

$4\frac{1}{2}$ oz (125 g) porridge oats
4 oz (110 g) butter (or margarine)
3 oz (75 g) demerara sugar

Pre-heat the oven to mark 5/375°F/190°C

Well butter a shallow baking tin (11×7 inches (28×18 cm)). Then melt 4 oz (110 g) of the butter gently in a saucepan, without letting it colour, and mix the sugar and porridge oats evenly in a mixing bowl. Now pour the melted butter into the mixture, and mix until all the ingredients are well and truly blended together. And all you have to do now is press this mixture all over the base of the baking tin and then bake in the oven for 15 minutes, or until they are a nice pale golden colour. Take the tin out of the oven, and cut the mixture into 12 portions—then leave in the tin until quite cold and crisp before removing them to an airtight tin (if you want to store them).

Butterfly Cakes   (To make about 18)

Very simple little cakes these, but it's amazing how quickly they disappear, especially if there are children around.

6 oz (175 g) self-raising flour
½ teaspoon baking powder
4 oz (110 g) caster sugar
4 oz (110 g) soft margarine
2 eggs, beaten
Coffee essence (i.e. Camp)
1 dessertspoon milk
A 5-fl oz (150-ml) carton double cream
Icing sugar

Pre-heat the oven to mark 5/375°F/190°C

Place the flour, baking powder, sugar, soft margarine, eggs, a dessertspoon of coffee essence and the milk in a large mixing bowl and whisk them together for about 1 minute, or until thoroughly blended. Now arrange 18 paper cake-cases in bun tins. Spoon about 1 heaped teaspoonful of cake mixture into each paper case, putting (as far as possible) an equal quantity of mixture in each case. Then bake in the top half of the oven for about 20 minutes, or until each cake is well risen and has stopped bubbling.

   Then remove the cakes to a wire rack to cool and, meanwhile, in a basin whip the cream with about a dessertspoon of coffee essence (or more if you prefer). Scoop a little cone off the top of each cake (a grapefruit knife is good for this), place a heaped teaspoon of cream in each cavity, then cut each little cone in half and arrange like butterfly wings on the top of the cream. Finally give them a light dusting of icing sugar and serve.

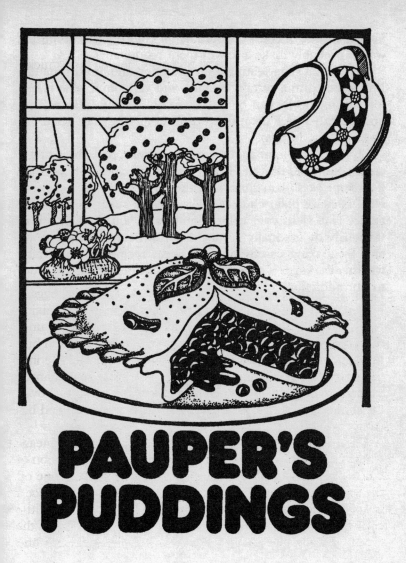

PAUPER'S PUDDINGS

One thing I've learned about nutritionists is that they rarely agree with each other. But since one thing they *do* agree about is that sugar (white or brown) is not necessary when people are eating normal balanced diets, I assume there is something in it. Dentists, of course, would ban it completely (except that would probably make a few of them redundant).

I agree that sugar-eating is an addiction and, unfortunately, I'm addicted to a certain extent—and very often what is bad for you medically can be good psychologically (it's amazing how quickly I perk up at the prospect of a Mars bar when I'm down in the dumps).

My real complaint about sugar in recipes, though, is that it can so easily kill flavour. Take chocolate recipes, for instance: if a recipe says plain chocolate, then it shouldn't say sugar as well, because plain chocolate already has sugar in it. So my advice is to slash your calorie intake and your budget simultaneously by gradually cutting down on sugar consumption and by looking carefully at all sweet recipes to determine whether the sugar is essential to the recipe or is there to pander to our addiction.

Honeycomb Mould
(Serves 4)

There are many commercial factory-made versions of this, but homemade it's so much nicer.

1 pint (570 ml) milk
Rind and juice of 2 lemons
3 eggs
3 oz (75g) granulated sugar
1½ level tablespoons gelatine powder

First place the milk in a saucepan with the thinly pared rind of the lemons. Bring slowly to the boil while separating the eggs into 2 basins. Then mix the sugar into the yolks. Strain the milk through a sieve on to the egg yolks and sugar, and whisk well before returning the mixture to the saucepan. Then stand the pan over a medium heat and stir until the liquid has almost reached boiling point and has thickened to a thinnish custard consistency. Now take the pan from the heat and leave it on one side to cool. Next sprinkle the gelatine into a small cup or basin containing 2 tablespoons of water. Leave it for a few minutes to give the gelatine time to soften, then place the cup in an inch (2.5 cm) of simmering water in a saucepan. Stir occasionally until the gelatine has dissolved and the liquid is absolutely clear. Then strain it into the cooling custard, mix thoroughly and, when the custard is cold, stir in the lemon juice. Now whisk the egg whites until stiff but not dry, and carefully fold them into the custard mixture. Pour the mixture into a 2½ pint (1.5-litre) basin and leave in a cool place to set—bearing in mind that it will separate into 3 layers: a clear jelly top, a creamy centre and a moussey base. Lovely!

Caramelised Apples

(Serves 4)

1½ lb (700 g) cooking apples
3 tablespoons water
A vanilla pod
½ oz (10 g) butter
1 tablespoon apricot jam
Sugar to taste

For the caramel:
3 oz (75 g) granulated sugar

Peel, core and slice the apples into a saucepan, add the water and vanilla pod, cover and cook very gently until the apples are soft. Then turn off the heat under the pan and remove the vanilla pod (which can be rinsed, dried and used again). Now add the butter and apricot jam to the pan and, after a minute or two, beat the mixture to a purée. Taste and add a bit more sugar if you think it needs it. Now spread the apple pulp in a heatproof bowl, cover and chill in the refrigerator.

To make the caramel, simply put the sugar in a saucepan and heat until it starts to dissolve around the edge and darken. Shake the pan gently and continue heating, stirring once or twice with a wooden spoon; continue to cook until the syrup formed is a shade darker than golden syrup. Now pour immediately over the apples and chill again until firm and cold. Tap the caramel surface all over with a spoon to break it up before serving—and some chilled 'real' custard would be lovely with it.

Rhubarb and Orange Flan   (Serves 6)

The orange in this recipe brings out the flavour of rhubarb beautifully.

For the pastry:
3 oz (75 g) fine oatmeal
5 oz (150 g) plain flour
2 teaspoons soft brown sugar
2 oz (50 g) lard
2 oz (50 g) butter

For the filling:
2 lb (900 g) rhubarb, trimmed, washed and cut into 1-inch (2.5 cm) chunks
3 oz (75 g) soft brown sugar
Rind and juice of 1 small orange
1 level tablespoon cornflour

Pre-heat the oven to mark 4/350°F/180°C

First of all place the rhubarb in a casserole, sprinkle it with the sugar, the orange zest and orange juice, and bake it uncovered for around 20–30 minutes, or until tender when tested with a skewer; then take it out of the oven and allow to cool. While it's cooling, make the pastry. Place the dry ingredients in a mixing bowl, rub in the fats to the fine 'breadcrumbs' stage, then add enough water to make a smooth dough. Roll it out and line an 8- or 9-inch (20- or 23-cm) flan tin with it (and reserve the pastry trimmings). Now prick the base and bake the flan case for about 25–30 minutes (temperatures as above); then remove it and increase the heat to mark 7/425°F/220°C. Meanwhile drain the rhubarb in a sieve placed over a bowl to reserve the juice, then mix the juice with the cornflour in a small saucepan until smooth, and simmer for 2 minutes. Now arrange the rhubarb in the cooked flan case, pour the sauce over and decorate the top with the pastry trimmings re-rolled and cut into thinnish strips ($\frac{1}{4}$ inch 5 mm wide) to make a sort of lattice-work pattern over the rhubarb. Now put it back into the oven and let it cook for a further 15 minutes. Serve warm with thick cream.

English Gooseberry Pie

Traditionally the first gooseberry pie of the season was always served on Whit Sunday—but, whenever it is, it's always something to look forward to each year.

2 lb (900 g) gooseberries
6 oz (175 g) sugar

For the pastry:
6 oz (175 g) plain flour
A pinch of salt
3 oz (75 g) lard
1 oz (25 g) margarine
A little milk

Pre-heat the oven to mark 7/425°F/220°C

For this you'll need a 1½-pint (850-ml) oval pie dish—or an oblong enamelled one of the same capacity. Just top and tail the gooseberries, then pile them into the pile dish and sprinkle the sugar in amongst them. Now make up the pastry by sifting the flour and salt together and rubbing the fats into it, then adding enough cold water to mix to a dough that leaves the bowl clean. Rest it for 20 minutes. Roll it out, cut a rim to fit the dish and dampen it. Press it in place, then dampen the rim and fit the lid on over it, knocking and fluting the edges. Make a steam hole (about the size of a 10p piece) in the centre, brush the surface of the pastry with milk and sprinkle just a trace more sugar over. Bake the pie in the oven for 10 minutes, then lower the heat to mark 5/375°F/190°C and bake for a further 30 minutes.

Spiced Bread and Apple Pudding

(Serves 4)

This is another useful way of using up stale bread, especially if you have a few windfall apples around.

About 5 or 6 medium slices wholemeal bread from a small loaf, buttered and with the crusts left on
2 medium cooking apples
1 oz (25 g) currants
1 teaspoon mixed spice
2 oz (50 g) demerara sugar
Freshly grated nutmeg
2 eggs
½ pint (275 ml) milk
A little butter

Pre-heat the oven to mark 4/350°F/180°C

First cut the slices of bread and butter in two, and arrange half of these (buttered side down) around the base of a 1½-pint (850-ml) baking dish. Sprinkle in half the currants, then peel and slice the apples (fairly thinly) and pile them in on top of the bread, sprinkling in the mixed spice and about two-thirds of the sugar. Now top with the rest of the pieces of bread (buttered side uppermost this time) and sprinkle in the rest of the currants and lots of freshly grated nutmeg and the rest of the sugar. Next whisk the eggs and beat them into the milk; pour this over everything, add a few flecks of butter, place the dish on the highest shelf of the oven and bake the pudding for about 30–40 minutes. The top will be golden and crusty and the underneath light and puffy; and, in my opinion, it doesn't need any cream.

Making Yoghurt at Home

Without going into all the bacteriological background of yoghurt cultures and so on, let me say just one thing: if you—and more important your family as well—eat yoghurt on a fairly regular basis, then it really is far cheaper to make it yourself (and far nicer to eat when it's homemade).

Having said that, however, I also think that making yoghurt without the help of a commercially designed yoghurt-maker is rather a hit-and-miss affair—inasmuch as you do need the right sort of 'warm place' and the correct type of ventilation etc. Therefore, I recommend you invest in a modest little yoghurt-making kit. There are many different types available.

Then, if you keep making yoghurt regularly, you'll never be short of a pudding course. I like thick yoghurt made with milk that has been reduced from 1 pint (570 ml) to about $\frac{3}{4}$ pint (420 ml) (by simmering for 25 minutes), chilled and then served with a dollop of runny honey—the way it's eaten in Greece. Similarly, it's delicious made into fruit yoghurts, with crushed soft fruits like strawberries, raspberries, red or blackcurrants or blackberries.

In the winter I make fruit yoghurt with chopped dried prunes or apricots, soaked then cooked, or I simply serve it with chopped apples, pears or oranges, or with a fruit salad. The variations are endless—no doubt you'll think of plenty of your own. But the marvellous thing about all of them is that they're so much better for us than all the starchy, sugary foods—and happily much cheaper!

Wholemeal Bread Pudding

(Serves 4)

6 oz (175 g) stale wholemeal bread, grated into crumbs (in a liquidiser)
8 fl oz (225 ml) milk
2 oz (50 g) currants
1 oz (25 g) raisins
1½ oz (40 g) candied peel, finely chopped
1½ oz (40 g) shredded suet
1½ oz (40 g) soft brown sugar
Grated rind of ½ lemon
Grated rind of ½ orange
1 level teaspoon mixed spice
½ level teaspoon ground cinnamon
¼ whole nutmeg, grated
1 large egg, beaten
A little butter

Put the breadcrumbs into a mixing bowl, pour the milk over them and mix thoroughly, then leave them to soak for about 30 minutes. Then stir in all the other ingredients, except for the butter, and mix very thoroughly. You should have a nice dropping consistency—if not, add a spot more milk. Finally spread the mixture evenly into a well-buttered 1- or 1½-pint (570- or 850-ml) baking dish and bake it at mark 4/350°F/180°C for about an hour.

Spotted Dick

(Serves 4)

A very comforting pudding this, especially with some warmed golden syrup poured over before serving.

8 oz (225 g) self-raising flour
A pinch salt
4 oz (110 g) butter
2 oz (50 g) caster sugar
6 oz (175 g) currants
2 medium eggs
A little milk
Some extra butter

First of all sift the flour and salt into a basin, and rub in the butter until the mixture looks nice and crumbly. Now stir in the sugar and the currants. Beat the eggs well, then add them a little at a time, stirring after each addition until the mixture is smooth. Add a little milk so that the mixture has a consistency where it will drop easily off the spoon. Pile the mixture into a 2-pint (1.2-litre) pudding basin (generously buttered) and cover with a sheet of greaseproof paper and a pleated sheet of foil. Tie securely with string, then steam in a steamer over simmering water for 2½ hours.

Prune and Apricot Jelly

(Serves 4)

Because homemade jelly is such a rarity I think this one is special enough to serve at a dinner party.

4 oz (110 g) dried prunes
4 oz (110 g) dried apricots
2 oz (50 g) sugar
1 small piece cinnamon stick
1 strip of orange peel
Juice of 1 orange
1 level tablespoon powdered gelatine

Start this off the night before by putting the dried prunes and apricots to soak in a pint (570 ml) of cold water. Then, when you're ready to make the jelly, pour the fruit (and the water they were soaked in) into a saucepan, adding the sugar, cinnamon and orange peel, and simmer gently for 20 minutes. Next fit a sieve over a bowl, pour the fruits into it and let them drain thoroughly. Then pour the liquid into a measuring jug, and add the orange juice and enough water to make it up to a pint (570 ml). At this stage taste to check there's enough sugar. Now put 3 tablespoons of the liquid into a small bowl, sprinkle in the gelatine and, when it has absorbed all the liquid, fit the bowl over a saucepan of barely simmering water. Stir now and then, and when the gelatine has dissolved and become quite transparent, strain it back into the rest of the mixture, mixing it in thoroughly. Now take the stones out of the prunes, and chop all the flesh of the fruits up roughly and arrange it in the base of a 2-pint (1.2-litre) mould. Pour the gelatine mixture over the fruit, and leave in a cool place to set.

Blackberry Cheese Cake (Serves 10)

This cheese cake will serve 10 people, or last a family a whole weekend, and using curd cheese instead of cream cheese makes it much more economical.

1 lb (450 g) curd cheese
4 medium eggs
1 teaspoon vanilla essence
5 oz (150 g) caster sugar
2 teaspoons lemon juice

For the base and topping:
8 gingernut biscuits
8 digestive biscuits
1 level teaspoon ground cinnamon
3 oz (75 g) butter melted
$\frac{3}{4}$ lb (350 g) blackberries
3 tablespoons caster sugar
2 teaspoons arrowroot mixed with 1 tablespoon water
1 extra digestive biscuit

Pre-heat the oven to mark 3/325°F/170°C

You will need an $8\frac{1}{2}$-inch (21.5-cm) cake tin with a loose base for this. Put the first lot of ingredients into a mixing bowl and whizz with an electric mixer until absolutely smooth. Then crush the 16 biscuits—a rolling pin and a flat surface will do it in seconds—scoop them into a bowl, and then mix with the cinnamon and the butter. Next press the biscuit mixture all over the base of the tin, bringing it up about $\frac{1}{2}$ inch (1 cm) at the edges. Pour the cheese mixture in now and bake for about 30–40 minutes, or until firm and set in the centre; then turn the oven off and leave the cheese cake there till cool. The black-berries should be washed and simmered with the caster sugar (but no water) for a very few minutes, then drained in a sieve over a bowl. Add the arrowroot-and-water mixture to the juice, bring to the boil and boil until thickened. Mix the thickened juice with the fruit and top the cake with the mixture when cool.

Press some more biscuit crumbs all round the edges. Serve only when thoroughly chilled.

Note: You can, of course, use other toppings. Blackcurrants are particularly nice, or fresh raspberries or strawberries—in season.

Spiced Apple Shortcake (Serves 6)

1½ lb (700 g) Bramley cooking apples
1 oz (25 g) soft brown sugar
¼ teaspoon ground cloves
1 teaspoon ground cinnamon
¼ whole nutmeg, grated
3 oz (75 g) sultanas
2 tablespoons water

For the topping:
8 oz (225 g) wholewheat flour
1 teaspoon baking powder
3 oz (75 g) butter
5 oz (150 g) soft brown sugar

Pre-heat the oven to mark 4/350°F/180°C

First quarter, core and peel the apples, then slice them thinly into a saucepan and mix them with the sugar, spices and sultanas; sprinkle with the water and cook gently until the apples are soft and fluffy. While that's happening, prepare the topping by mixing the flour and baking powder in a bowl. Now rub the fat into the flour until the mixture becomes crumbly. Then stir in the sugar, making sure that all the lumps are broken down. Next arrange the apple mixture in a 4-pint (2.25-litre) pie (or baking) dish. Sprinkle the crumble mixture lightly over this and bake in the oven for 30 minutes. Serve either warm or cold.

Traditional Lemon Pancakes   (Serves 4)

4 oz (110 g) plain flour
A pinch of salt
2 eggs
7 fl oz (200 ml) milk and 3 fl oz (75 ml) water (mixed together)
2 tablespoons melted butter
Some lard
4 large lemons
Some caster sugar
A 7- or 8-inch heavy frying pan

Begin by sifting the flour and salt into a bowl, and making a well in the centre. Break the eggs into this well, then whisk the eggs incorporating a little of the flour as you do so. Then when the mixture starts to get too thick, begin adding the milk-and-water mixture a little at a time—still whisking—until it's all in and you have a smooth batter with the consistency of thin cream.

Then when you are ready to cook the pancakes, add the melted butter to the batter, and have ready a couple of plates warming in the oven (if you pop the lemons in as well, they'll squeeze more easily). Now melt a little lard in the frying pan, swirling it around to coat the whole pan and the sides and pouring out any excess fat (into a saucer). When the pan is smoking hot, pour in 2 tablespoons of batter and turn the heat down to medium. Tip the pan from side to side to make sure the batter covers the whole base and when the pancake is brown on the underneath, flip it over with a palette knife and brown the other side. Then keep it warm between your two hot plates while you're making the remainder. Serve with lemon squeezed over and some sugar sprinkled on, and roll up.

Spiced Apricot Compote (Serves 3)

Unless you're lucky enough to get your apricots picked warm from the tree, I think gentle cooking gives them much more flavour.

1 lb (450 g) fresh apricots (approximately 9), slightly under-
   ripe is better
2 tablespoons dark soft brown sugar
$\frac{1}{2}$ pint (275 ml) hot water
1 small piece cinnamon stick
1 vanilla pod
2 teaspoons arrowroot

Pre-heat the oven to mark 3/325°F/160°C

First place the apricots, sugar, water and spices in a thick cooking pot (earthenware is ideal), cover them tightly, place in the oven and let them cook for about $\frac{3}{4}$–1 hour depending on their ripeness—they need to be cooked until tender but not disintegrating. When they're cooked, remove the apricots to a serving dish using a draining spoon. Then pour the juices into a small saucepan and extract the spices. Now bring the juices up to simmering point, mix the arrowroot with 1 tablespoon of cold water till smooth, add it to the juices, bring back to simmering point and continue to simmer until the mixture has thickened to a syrupy consistency. Then pour the sauce over the apricots and serve either warm or chilled.

CONVERSION TABLES

All these are approximate conversions, which have either been rounded up or down. In a few recipes it has been necessary to modify them very slightly. Never mix metric and imperial measures in one recipe, stick to one system or the other. All spoon measurements used throughout this book are level unless specified otherwise.

OVEN TEMPERATURES		
Mark 1	275	140
2	300	150
3	325	170
4	350	180
5	375	190
6	400	200
7	425	220
8	450	230
9	475	240

WEIGHTS	
$\frac{1}{2}$oz	10 g
$\frac{3}{4}$	20
1	25
$1\frac{1}{2}$	40
2	50
$2\frac{1}{2}$	60
3	75
4	110
$4\frac{1}{2}$	125
5	150
6	175
7	200
8	225
9	250
10	275
12	350
1lb	450
$1\frac{1}{2}$	700
2	900
3	1.35 kg

MEASUREMENTS	
$\frac{1}{8}$ inch	3mm
$\frac{1}{4}$	5 mm
$\frac{1}{2}$	1 cm
$\frac{3}{4}$	2
1	2.5
$1\frac{1}{4}$	3
$1\frac{1}{2}$	4
$1\frac{3}{4}$	4.5
2	5
$2\frac{1}{2}$	6
3	7.5
$3\frac{1}{2}$	9
4	10
5	13
$5\frac{1}{4}$	13.5
6	15
$6\frac{1}{2}$	16
7	18
$7\frac{1}{2}$	19
8	20
9	23
$9\frac{1}{2}$	24
10	25.5
11	28
12	30

VOLUME	
2 fl oz	55 ml
3	75
5 ($\frac{1}{4}$pt)	150
$\frac{1}{2}$pt	275
1	570
$1\frac{1}{4}$	725
$1\frac{3}{4}$	1 litre
2	1.2
$2\frac{1}{2}$	1.5
4	2.25

INDEX

anchovies:
  tomato and anchovy
    quiche, 170
  with baked fish and
    potatoes, 57
  with egg salad, 44
  with spaghetti and olives,
    164
apples:
  caramelised, 210
  pork rissoles with spiced
    apple sauce, 90
  spiced bread pudding,
    213
  spiced shortcake, 219
apricots:
  and prune jelly, 217
  spiced compote, 221

bacon:
  boiled, with pease
    pudding, 104
  with dumplings, parsley
    sauce, 101–102
  pie with egg, 40
baking, 195–196
beans:
  Boston baked, 185
  haricot and lentil chilli,
    191–192
  white, and salami salad,
    188–189
beef:
  baked stuffed cabbage
    leaves, 108
  brown stew with
    dumplings, 95–96
  in cider, 87

Cornish pasties
  (traditional), 105
curry, 99
steak and kidney hotpot,
  106
steak and onion in
  Guinness, 97
stew with tomato, 107
offal
ox liver and vegetable
  hotpot, 117
oxtail braised in cider, 122
oxtail hotpot, 120
biscuits, oat crunch, 205
bread:
  Irish soda, 199
  sticky tea, 198
  quick wholemeal, 202

cakes:
  butterfly, 206
  date, prune and walnut
    loaf, 203
  orange and sultana
    (sugarless), 200
  seed (old-fashioned), 204
  shortbread, wheatmeal,
    201
  strawberry jam sponge, 197
  cereals, 155–156, 157–165
chick peas:
  chicken and, 74–75
  salad, 184
  spiced cutlets, 187
chicken, 69–70, 71–81
  Catalane, 72
  chick peas and, 74–75
  drumsticks, devilled, 73

mustard-coated, 77
pilau, spiced, 76
pot roast, 71
southern fried, 75
spiced with lentils, 78
cider, 17, 80, 87, 122, 133,
  136
cream, 17–18
curries:
  dhal, 186
  eggs with cauliflower, 177
  egg patties, 37
  egg patties with lentil, 190
  ground beef, 99
  vegetable, 193

eggs, 35–36, 37–49
  au gratin with cauliflower
    and celery, 43–44
  baked with potato and
    cheese, 45
  cheese soufflé, 41
  curried patties, 37
  curried patties with lentils,
    190
  curried with cauliflower,
    177
  omelette with bacon, leek,
    potato, 47
  omelette piperade, 49
  pie with bacon, 40
  poached with spinach
    soufflé, 42–43
  poached with Welsh rarebit
    soufflé, 38
  salad with anchovy, 44–45
  Savoyard, 46
  Spanish tortilla, 48

with cheese and spinach
  sauce, 39
energy saving, 15–16

fish, 51–52, 53–67
  anchovy and tomato
    quiche, 66–67
  baked with potatoes and
    anchovies, 57
  fish cakes with capers, 60
  fish cakes, salmon, 64
  herrings with caper
    stuffing, 62
  herrings fried in oatmeal,
    55
  herrings, soused, 54–55
  kipper quiche, 63
  mackerels with caper
    sauce, 66
  mackerels, marinaded, 65
  mackerels en papillote, 58
  mackerels with rhubarb
    sauce, 59
  soufflé, 56
  sprats, deep fried, mustard
    sauce, 61–62
  whiting au gratin, 53
flans:
  spinach cream, 174–175
  wholewheat, cheese and
    vegetable, 172–173
  sweet
  rhubarb and orange, 211
frankfurters:
  German soup with, 25
  with hot potato salad,
    132
frozen food, 14–15

gammon: 'Fidget pie', 100

herbs, 16

lamb:
  baked stuffed breast, 89
  navarin, 102
  stuffed shoulder with rice
    and olives, 91
  roast with coriander, 86
  offal
  hearts, stuffed and braised,
    111–112
  kidneys with chipolatas,
    116
  kidneys in gravy, 121
  kidneys spiced in yoghurt,
    113
  kidneys Stroganoff, 114
  kidney-stuffed onions,
    119
  liver and bacon kebabs
    with stuffing, 115
  liver casserole, 123
  liver with crisp-fried
    onions, 118
  liver and onion Yorkshire
    pudding, 124
lentils:
  Chilladas, 183
  chilli with haricot beans,
    191–192
  dhal curry, 186
  patties curried with egg,
    190
  salad, bean and anchovy,
    189–190
  with spiced chicken, 78

  with split pea loaf, 191
  with vegetable curry, 193

macaroni:
  au gratin, 165
  carbonara, 163
marrows, 142
  baked with sage and
    cheese, 179
  with tomatoes and
    coriander, 150
meat, 83–84, 85–108
mutton pot pie, 94

noodles, buttered, with meat
    balls, 160

offal, 109–110, 111–126
oil, 16–17

pancakes:
  with spinach and cheese,
    178
  traditional lemon, 220
pease pudding, 104
pies:
  egg and bacon, 40
  Fidget pie, 100
  leek, carrot, potato, 176
  mutton pot, 94
  sweet
  English gooseberry, 212
pizza:
  cream cheese, olives,
    anchovies, 170–171
  dough, 169
  salami and mushrooms,
    171

pork:
  'au chou', 96–97
  braised with prunes, 85
  chops boulangère, 103
  devilled slices, 98
  hotpot with kidney, 88
  pot roast with cabbage and
    juniper, 92
  rissoles with spiced apple
    sauce, 90
  with summer vegetables,
    93
  offal
  pig's liver faggots and peas,
    125–126
  kidneys with mustard
    cream sauce, 112–113
puddings, 207–208, 209–221
  blackberry cheese cake,
    218–219
  caramelised apples, 210
  English gooseberry pie,
    212
  honeycomb mould, 209
  lemon pancakes
    (traditional), 220
  prune and apricot jelly, 217
  rhubarb and orange flan,
    211
  spiced apple shortcake,
    219
  spiced apricot compote,
    221
  'Spotted Dick' pudding,
    215
  wholemeal bread pudding,
    215
pulses, 181–182, 183–193

quiches, 5
  kipper, 63
  tomato and anchovy, 66–
    67

rabbit:
  in cider, 80
  harvest, 79–80
  roasted with onions and
    bacon, 81
rice:
  (brown) salad, 158
  (brown) with vegetables,
    159
  onion, 157
  onion with herbs, 157
  spiced pilau, 157
  spiced pilau, chicken,
    76

salads:
  brown rice, 158
  broad bean, 143
  chick peas, 184
  egg and anchovy, 44–45
  hot potato, 132
  lentil, bean and anchovy,
    189–190
  white bean and salami,
    188–189
sauces:
  caper, 66
  cheese and spinach, 39
  chilli, 130
  cider, 136
  mustard, 61
  mustard cream, 112
  parsley, 101

rhubarb, 59
spiced apple, 90
tomato and chilli, 145
sausages, 127–128, 129–139
    boulangère, 137
    braised in cider, 133
    Cassoulet ('Poor Man's'),
        139
    frankfurters with hot
        potato salad, 132
    home-made, 129
    stuffing for onions, 130–
        131
    toad-in-the-hole with sage
        and onions, 134
    with chilli sauce, 130
    with cider sauce, 136
    with lentils, 135
    with purée of peas, 138
soufflés:
    cheese, 41
    courgette, 173–174
    fish, 56
    jacket potatoes, 152
    spinach and poached egg,
        42–43
    Welsh rarebit with poached
        eggs, 38
soups, 19–20, 21–33
    basic stock, 21
    carrot and leek, 30
    cauliflower, 32
    celery, cream of, 29
    chou (soupe au), 33
    country, thick, 24
    Flamande (potage), 27
    German, with frankfurters,
        25

goulash with dumplings,
    22
Les Halles, 26
paysanne (potage), 28
potato with bacon, 31
split pea and vegetable, 23
spaghetti:
    Bolognese, 161–162
    with meat balls, 160–161
    with olives and anchovies,
        164
    with tuna and olives, 162
spices, 16
sugar, 207–208

TVP (textured vegetable
    protein), 83, 181–182

vegetables, 14, 141–142, 143–
    154
    aubergines, baked, 144
    broad bean salad, 143
    'bubble and squeak', 154
    cabbage (white) with garlic
        and coriander, 146
    courgettes à la grecque, 148
    marrow baked with sage
        and cheese, 179
    marrow with tomatoes and
        coriander, 150
    parsnips, purée of, 149
    potatoes (new) with bacon
        and onion, 151
    potatoes, Irish, 153
    potatoes, jacket, soufflé,
        152
    swedes, mashed with
        bacon, 147

tomatoes, chilli sauce, 145
turnips boulangère, 146–147

vegetarian dishes, 167–168, 169–179

weights and measures 223
wine, 17

yoghurt:
    spiced kidneys in, 113
    home-made, 214

NOTES

NOTES

NOTES

NOTES

NOTES

NOTES

NOTES

NOTES

NOTES